Senior Executive Reward

Senior Executive Reward

Key Models and Practices

SANDY PEPPER

GOWER

Published by
Gower Publishing Limited
Gower House
Croft Road
Aldershot
Hampshire
GU11 3HR
England

Gower Publishing Company
Suite 420
101 Cherry Street
Burlington
VT 05401-4405
USA

Alexander (Sandy) Pepper has asserted his moral right under the Copyright, Designs and Patents Act, 1988, to be identified as the author of this work.

British Library Cataloguing in Publication Data
Pepper, Sandy
    Senior executive reward: key models and practices
    1.Executives – Salaries, etc.
    I.Title
    658.4'0722

    ISBN-10: 0 566 08733 2
    ISBN-13: 978-0-566-08733-2

Library of Congress Control Number: 2006926066

Printed and bound in Great Britain by MPG Books Ltd., Bodmin, Cornwall

Contents

List of Figures

List of Tables

The value, or WORTH of a man, is as of all other things, his price; that is to say, so much as would be given for the use of his power: and is therefore not absolute; but a thing dependent on the need and judgement of another. An able conductor of soldiers, is of great price in time of war present, or imminent; but in peace not so. A learned and uncorrupt judge, is much worth in time of peace; but not so much in war. As in other things, so in men, not the seller, but the buyer determines the price. For let a man, as most men do, rate themselves at the highest value they can; yet their true value is no more than it is esteemed by others.

Thomas Hobbes (1651) *Leviathan*, Part 1, Chapter X.

Foreword

No one doubts that we live in an age of ever-increasing litigiousness. Although in the United Kingdom we have not yet achieved the height of the art as practised by our cousins in the United States, a compensation culture has grown to far beyond where it was only ten or twenty years ago. Nowadays, blame is an automatic reaction to loss. Not self-blame, or even an acceptance of the old adage of caveat emptor, but the immediate conclusion that someone else must be at fault. There must be someone to sue.

Couple that development with the fact that the media have become our watchdogs and are faster to exploit the possible deficiencies of others and, even more and quite rightly, any suspected acts of omission or commission, deliberate or otherwise. Often, long-cultured reputations are suddenly sullied, or at worst, ruined, long before any proof of guilt is actually achieved. What used to be a little reported sideline, breaches in corporate governance are now described as scandals, and corporate failure leads to a search for blame. Even without an accompanying financial disaster, and however much the editors of the popular tabloids may be paid, the phrase 'noses in the trough' has become a regular headline when corporate pay for senior executives is discussed. The press treat the vast pay of footballers and pop singers as the result of quite normal market forces, but the incentive awards of CEOs and other senior executives are regarded as 'obscene' at levels a fraction of their younger high earners. Since these are facts of life, it is better for those determining the pay of executives to be forewarned and forearmed.

The press accepts the vast pay of footballers and pop singers, but finds the incentive awards of CEOs 'obscene'.

It is said there was an age when, at a certain time in the later life of a successful mogul of industry, retired senior civil servant or politician, a seat on the board was an expected step between achievement and retirement. It was not expected to be hard work, after all, and what could be better than to serve as a non-executive director at the pinnacle of a major corporation, where the actual executives – gifted, younger, still striving – are creating the wealth for shareholders, the staff and the national economy? Generously rewarded, little actual responsibility, the company of friends (the greatest of whom were the chairman and the managing director) was a life for five or ten years or so which one had earned. A long luncheon every two months or so, with the finest of wines, would follow the board meeting. After all, the auditors would get the numbers right, the company secretary would deal with all those legal things and the chairman knew what he was doing.

If it was ever like that, how times have changed! Massive corporate disasters (the most recent in a long line being the oft quoted Enron, WorldCom and Parmalat) show that this is now an international dilemma, leading to criminal charges of many concerned and even the collapse of one of the largest accounting firms in the world. Being a director is now, as actually it always was in truth, a very great responsibility.

Corporate governance is the prime proactive duty of the whole board – jointly and severally. An independent director must truly be so: independent in thought, word and deed from the CEO, who in turn increasingly holds an entirely separate set of responsibilities from the chairman. There are also board committees to serve upon, with specific duties of oversight and accountability. There was, just a few months ago, a cartoon depicting Jersey Zoo, founded by the late Gerald Durrell to preserve endangered species. One of the cages bore a sign 'audit committee chairman'! But thanks to the City and its equivalent in other major economies, these matters are now taken very seriously, with successive codes of conduct, such that investors, lenders, lawyers, accountants and boards themselves are better educated as to the current responsibilities of directors. No longer the preserve of the gifted amateur, the modern director has to be professionally minded, properly trained and aware of the great trust he has to exercise in preserving the company's assets.

No longer the preserve of the gifted amateur, the modern director has to be professionally minded and properly trained.

One such new set of skills is demonstrated clearly in the development of the remuneration committee. Instead of merely requiring judgement, the members of this committee now need a far more scientific basis for their deliberations. There is a bewildering array of competing mathematical theories required in the calculation of what the Americans call 'compensation'. There is also a greater sophistication in the types of payment that should be considered for executives, not only for basic pay, but to encourage retention and performance. I have served on five remuneration committees, and the mental processes get ever more complicated with each one.

Sandy Pepper is a brilliant chartered accountant and management consultant of the modern school. (Incidentally, I once taught him company law!) A specialist in all aspects of corporate pay, he has neatly summarised all the current legal and practical requirements to be considered by directors in exercising their responsibilities. To what extent should one refer to and rely upon the fashionable industry percentiles of the myriad of consulting firms? What goals should be set to maximise the performance of the executives? He has provided the full range of theories. Most of all he has recognised the human element – the psychology involved when one is determining the pay of people who are colleagues.

The Rt. Hon. Sir Jeremy Hanley, KCMG

Acknowledgements

Many of my friends and colleagues have given help, advice and encouragement to me while writing this book. My thanks in particular go to Helen Bromley, Michael Bursee, John Caplan, Ron Collard, Tom Gosling, Michael Jaffe, Robert Kuipers, Scott Olsen, Kirsten Palmer-Jeffery and Leyla Yildirim. There are many others who I have omitted from this list, but not forgotten.

Thanks also go to Jonathan Norman, Fiona Martin and others at Gower Publishing for their guidance, insights and for the opportunity they have given me.

Jeremy Hanley has written a foreword that is both instructive and entertaining, as I remember his law lectures used to be! I am very grateful for his support.

Finally, and closer to home, my love and thanks go to Deborah, Alistair, Simon and Robert for putting up with me while I have been writing this book – I hope they think it is worth it!

CHAPTER 1

Introduction

PURPOSE OF THIS BOOK

Books, articles and academic papers on executive remuneration have become increasingly common in the last ten years. They are written by economists, lawyers, consultants and journalists. You find them in newspapers, business weeklies, human resources (HR) practitioner magazines and academic journals. They fall into various categories. Some are sensationalist, others apologetic. Some are highly theoretical and beyond the reach of those without an extensive knowledge of economics.[1] Few achieve a balance, combining a practical view with an intellectual underpinning. That is the objective of this book: to explain in an intelligent, unsensational and balanced way how modern executives are paid – and why.

The executive pay question has many facets. Consider the following. Why has executive pay increased so much since the early 1990s? Why is executive compensation, as they call it in the US, typically higher than it is in the UK, which in turn is generally higher than the rest of Europe? Why is the average remuneration of executives in France higher than it is in Germany? Why are Swiss executive reward levels comparable only to those found in the US? Why are equity plans uncommon in Japan? Why have some companies discovered that their long-term incentive plans pay out significant sums at times when their share price is falling? Why have remuneration committees recommended pay proposals which have subsequently been roundly rejected by shareholders? Why are details of directors' pay disclosed in great detail in the UK while many German companies still resist giving such information?

During the course of this book I will try to answer these specific questions. At the same time I will address the biggest question of all: is it possible to reach an equilibrium point – where senior executives are generally happy with their

Is it possible to reach an equilibrium point, where senior executives, shareholders and companies are happy?

---

1   For the most famous example of sensationalist literature on executive compensation see Crystal, G.S. (1991), *In Search of Excess: The Overcompensation of American Executives*, W.W. Norton & Co, New York.

pay, shareholders are generally happy with what their senior executives are being paid, and companies believe their leaders are properly motivated and incentivised?

BASIC MODEL

The conceptual framework used here is the consultant's four-box model (see Figure 1). It groups the issues into four categories. The first two categories, in the top left- and right-hand boxes, deal with economic models, psychology, sociology and organisational behaviour. These are the more theoretical parts of our examination of executive reward – the parts most commonly the subject of academic research. In the bottom left- and right-hand boxes are tax and accounting on the one hand, and corporate governance on the other. These are the more practical aspects of our examination: the domain of practitioners – compensation and benefits specialists, lawyers, accountants and so on. Looking at it in a different way, the left-hand column focuses primarily on financial issues; the right hand column focuses primarily on behaviours.

Summary:
This book looks at the theory (economic and behavioural) and the practice (tax, accounting and corporate governance) that inform decisions about executive pay.

	More focused on financial issues	*More focused on behavioural issues*
More theoretical	Economic models	Psychology, sociology and organisational behaviour
More practical	Tax and accounting	Corporate governance

Figure 1 Factors determining senior executive reward

The four categories, proceeding clockwise from the top left-hand corner, are each the subject of a separate chapter. The aim of the final chapter is to bring the various ideas together into a single set of principles and best practices.

TWO ASSUMPTIONS

Before we begin we need to make two key assumptions that underpin the analysis which will follow in subsequent chapters.

The first assumption is about the nature of humankind: what causes us to do the things that we do? The economists' traditional assumption is that people are rational and self-interested. They take actions with the intention of maximising personal utility, typically thought of primarily in monetary terms, and over the short run in preference to the long run. A more sophisticated approach is proposed by Michael C. Jensen of Harvard Business School. Jensen proposes that people are resourceful, evaluative and maximising:[2] they are clever and creative; they want more of the things that they value rather than less; they make choices, trade-offs and substitutions; they seek to maximise the value of their goods, meaning here the things that they value, be they tangible or intangible.

People are both rational and irrational... psychological factors are at play as well as reason when it comes to executive pay.

Though persuasive in many ways, the resourceful, evaluative and maximising model of human behaviour is still deficient in one important respect: it rests on the presumption that people are always rational, and we know that this is not the case. People are both rational and irrational. There is a double loop in our mental processes: two sets of systems, one logical, the other psychological, are intertwined. We are resourceful, capable of evaluating situations and making choices. We are also emotional. We have needs. We are affected by the social environment in which we live. We are capable of acting altruistically as well as selfishly. At times we do things which even we cannot really explain. This model of human behaviour, a dualistic model which recognises that there are psychological factors at play as well as reason, is the one we shall assume as we examine various aspects of executive pay.

The second assumption is in response to the question 'What is a company for?' The often repeated phrase 'to maximise shareholder value' is in many ways inadequate because it places too little emphasis on the legitimate interests of other stakeholders – lenders, customers, employees and so on. The problem with stakeholder theory, which tries to embrace these other perspectives too, is that it fails to provide satisfactory mechanisms for evaluating the competing demands of different interests, leaving senior management unable to make purposeful decisions. A better view is what Michael Jensen and Kevin J. Murphy of the Marshall Business School at the University of Southern California call 'enlightened value maximisation' or 'enlightened stakeholder theory', which proposes that the proper objective of a company is to create (and ultimately to maximise) the long-run total value of the firm.[3]

---

2   Jensen, M.C. (1998), *Foundations of Organisational Strategy*, Harvard University Press, Cambridge, Massachusetts.

3   Jensen, M.C. and Murphy, K.J. (2004), *Remuneration: Where We've Been, How We Got Here, What Are the Problems, and How to Fix Them*, European Corporate Governance Institute Working Paper No. 44/2004.

Note the two important elements of this way of answering the question:

- Value is to be maximised in the long run, not the short run;
- It is firm value not shareholder value which is to be maximised.

This admits the legitimate interest in value creation of at least some other stakeholders, including top management and other employees. It is now widely accepted that, just as shareholders contribute financial capital to a firm, so management and employees contribute human capital, being the sum total of their knowledge, skill, experience, intelligence and so on. There are various ways of placing a value on human capital: for example, as a minimum (looking at it solely from the executive's perspective) the human capital of a company's chief executive officer (CEO) might be calculated as the net present value of his expected future earnings from his or her best alternative source of employment.

The enlightened value maximisation assumption can itself be derived from one of the fundamental principles of social welfare: society's object is to maximise total utility, to create the greatest good for the greatest number, and to maximise the efficiency with which society uses resources to create wealth and minimise waste. What it does not do, however, is deal with the question of how value is to be allocated between different stakeholders, which is not a straightforward matter.

Although different stakeholders all have a legitimate interest in the value created by a firm, this does not mean that their interests are equal. One way of looking at the problem of allocation between stakeholders is like this. The interests of some stakeholders might be satisfied if they are simply kept happy, without direct financial compensation; this might be true, for example, for customers and for society in general. The interests of other stakeholders might be satisfied by a fixed-rate return; for example lenders and junior employees who are content to be remunerated solely by wages or salary – a fixed rate for the job in question. Some stakeholders, however, require an equity return – a share in profits – because they share a proportionate amount of risk; this includes not only shareholders, but also top management, given the amount of the human capital they have invested and the risks they run if things do not turn out for the best.

TWO DEFINITIONS

As well as making two assumptions, we also need two important definitions.

The first is what is meant by 'senior executive'. Many books and articles on executive remuneration concentrate on the CEO. But a lot of the issues which apply to CEOs are common to a broader group of senior executives, including the chief operating officer (COO), chief financial officer (CFO), chief technology officer, head of sales and marketing, human resource director and

Although different stakeholders have a legitimate interest in the value created by a firm, this does not mean their interests are equal.

so on. In the US this group is sometimes referred to as the 'C suite'; in the UK and Europe, the 'executive committee', 'general management committee' or 'executive board'; in France, the '*directoire*'; in Germany, the '*Vorstand*'; and so on. Changing trends in corporate governance mean that, while historically in the US and UK many of these individuals would have been main-board executive directors, it is increasingly common to find only the CEO and CFO on the main board. In Continental Europe, where it has been more common to separate supervisory and executive functions into a two-tier board structure, it is the executive board we are talking about. In short, we are focusing on the group of very senior executives responsible for defining and executing a company's strategy, who through their actions are capable of directly affecting (positively or negatively) the company's profits, share price, reputation, market positioning and so on.

By 'senior executive remuneration', we mean the total reward of key executives who are responsible for defining and executing a company's strategy.

The second definition we need is what we mean by 'executive remuneration' – what the Americans call compensation or what might more commonly in Europe now be referred to as reward. Most executive pay packages contain four basic components: a base salary, an annual bonus typically tied to financial performance, an equity plan or some other type of long-term incentive arrangement, and a retirement scheme. In addition, executives participate in broad-based employee benefit plans and they may also receive special benefits, including enhanced life insurance and medical plans, use of corporate jets and chauffeur-driven cars. There may be other special terms of employment: for example, in the US the provision of formal employment contracts in contrast to the employment-at-will arrangements applicable to other staff. In the UK and Europe the special employment terms might include relatively long notice periods to protect the executives in the event of redundancy (though new corporate governance regulations are increasingly placing limits on long notice periods). Practitioners now refer to this bundle of rights, monetary and non-monetary, as 'total reward', and it is that which is the subject of this book.

NOTE ON CASE STUDIES

This book contains a number of case studies and other examples which are intended to illustrate the main concepts that are being described. None of these cases are fictional; most are drawn from public information sources, and only a few involve private knowledge. Nevertheless, in all instances I have tried as far as possible to make the cases anonymous while at the same time remaining true to the underlying facts. My reasons for this approach are various. In particular, my intention is not to comment on or criticise any particular company: other examples could equally well have been used. I am also well aware that there may be other relevant facts and circumstances, not obvious at first sight, which might explain the actions taken.

CHAPTER 2

Compensation, Benefits and Incentives

This chapter describes the basic elements of executive reward – a base salary, an annual bonus, a long-term incentive payable in cash, shares or share options, a pension, and other benefits which may be delivered as cash allowances or in non-cash form. Compensation specialists and others with a good basic knowledge of executive compensation can if they wish move directly to Chapter 3. Others should read on. Note that much of the basic analysis contained in the first part of this chapter is based on the academic work of Kevin Murphy.[1]

SALARIES

Base salaries for senior executives are typically determined by benchmarking using salary surveys, often categorised by size of company and industry and supplemented by detailed analysis of comparator companies. Since salaries below the median are often labelled as below market, while those in the top two quartiles are considered to be competitive, the survey approach has contributed to a ratcheting-up effect in base salary levels over the years. Pay surveys do not generally take account of other criteria which many economists consider relevant for predicting earnings levels, including previous experience, qualifications and so on. Moreover, company size is at best an imperfect proxy for managerial skill requirements, job complexity and span of control.

Companies devote a significant amount of time to the salary determination process, even though salaries comprise a decreasing proportion of total compensation.

Companies devote a significant amount of time to the salary determination process, even though salaries comprise a decreasing proportion of total compensation. There are a number of reasons for this:

• Base salaries are a key component of executive employment contracts and a reference point for many other elements of reward: target annual

---

1 Murphy, K.J. (1999), 'Executive Compensation', in O. Ashenfelter and D. Card (eds) *Handbook of Labor Economics* (Vol. 3), North Holland, Amsterdam.

bonuses are often defined as a percentage or multiple of base salary; defined pension benefits and severance arrangements also typically depend on salary levels;

- Senior executives who, like many other individuals, are often naturally risk averse will frequently prefer an increase in base salary to a corresponding increase in target bonuses or other variable compensation.

SHORT-TERM INCENTIVES

Annual bonus contracts are generally explicitly set out in a contract or plan, with at most a limited role for discretion. In some firms, boards can exercise discretion in allocating a fixed bonus pool among participating executives, but the flexibility in these cases affects only individual allocations and not the overall amount of the payout. Otherwise, discretion is often limited to the part it plays in the assessment of an executive's performance and in determining whether performance standards have been met.

Annual bonus plans come in many different forms. Key elements of design are the performance threshold or trigger point, the level of the bonus cap if any, and the performance standard which is used. Under what Kevin Murphy calls an '80/120' plan no bonus is paid unless performance exceeds, say, 80% of the performance standard and bonuses are capped once performance exceeds, say, 120% of the performance standard. The actual percentages vary from company to company and plan to plan. Performance standards which are budget based are common, but create incentives for executives to manipulate the budget process and to avoid actions in the current year that might have an undesirable effect on next year's budget. Similarly, prior-year performance standards can cause a ratcheting-down effect, since managers know that good current performance will be penalised in the next period through an enhanced performance standard. In contrast, absolute standards, for example based on cost of capital or the comparative performance of an index or industry peer group, are not as easily influenced by the participants and have many advantages, though care must be taken when absolute standards are initially set or the external peer group is defined.

Key elements of annual bonus design are the performance threshold, the level of bonus cap and the performance standard.

Unfortunately the incentive effect of an annual bonus is not consistent throughout the range of company performance as Figure 2 shows. For example, if year-to-date performance suggests that the bonus cap will be readily achieved (in Figure 2 if performance is expected to reach P_3), then executives may withhold effort in an attempt to defer earnings for use in subsequent years. Equally, if year-to-date performance is significantly below the incentive zone (if performance is well below P_1), then managers may discount the bonus opportunity altogether. If expected performance is marginally below the performance threshold (just below P_1) then the discontinuity in the level of bonus payments at the threshold level yields strong incentives to achieve the performance standard. The rate of change of the slope of the pay–performance curve at the threshold level is effectively infinite. This may (both desirably and legitimately) result in increased effort, but more dangerously might lead to undue risk taking or even an attempt to manipulate earnings by creative accounting. These discontinuity characteristics are exaggerated further if the bonus plan proceeds in steps rather than in a straight line (see, for example, the step function represented by the dashed line running from P_1R_1 to P_3R_3 in Figure 2).

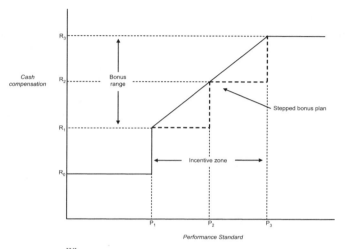

Where:

    R_0 = Base salary immediately before performance threshold

    R_1 = Base salary plus bonus at performance threshold (P_1)

    R_2 = Base salary plus target bonus at target performance level (P_2)

    R_3 = Base salary plus maximum bonus at performance ceiling (P_3)

Figure 2 Typical annual bonus plan (after Murphy, 1999)

Annual bonus plans for senior executives typically use accounting measures (growth in profits, profit margins, earnings per share and so on) as the basis of their performance standards. Accounting data is easily verifiable and widely understood. However, there are two fundamental problems:

- Accounting results are inherently backward looking and short run; this means that executives may choose to avoid actions which reduce current profits but would enhance future profitability, for example capital investment or research and development expenditure;
- It is an unfortunate fact that accounting profits can sometimes be manipulated, for example by creatively managing expense accruals or by shifting revenues between accounting periods.

STOCK OPTIONS

For many years the most common way of providing long-term incentives has been in the form of stock options. Stock options are contracts which give the option-holder the right to buy shares at an agreed price (the exercise or strike price) at some future date. Most commonly, the exercise price is the market value of the underlying shares at the grant date, the date that options are awarded. Executive share options vest over time, either progressively (for example 25% per year over four years) or all at one time (cliff vesting) after, say, three years. Executive options are generally non-transferable, non-tradable, and expire if they have not been exercised by, say, the tenth anniversary of the date of grant. The terms on which options are granted will typically specify what happens if the executive leaves the firm before the options have vested. Good leavers (executives who leave because of ill-health, redundancy or early retirement) may be allowed to exercise their options, whereas bad leavers (executives who leave of their own volition or are dismissed for cause) are not allowed to do this. The stock plan may also specify what happens in the event of a takeover or merger of the company: options may vest automatically on a change of control, or may be rolled over into shares in the acquiring company.

Different types of options

Variations include premium options (granted with a strike price which is higher than the share value at the grant date), nil-cost options (where the strike price is set at a nominal amount) and variable price options (where the exercise price varies, for example by being linked to an average share price index). The rate at which options vest may be subject to a performance condition, for example requiring the company's earnings per share to grow at a particular rate before options become exercisable. In some countries, including the US and the UK, options satisfying certain conditions may be given favourable tax status, known as qualified or approved options, as opposed to non-qualified or unapproved options which do not have special tax treatment. Re-load options are options granted under a plan which provides that the number of shares under option is automatically topped up to the previous levels if an option is exercised in full or in part.

The popularity of stock options in the past has in large part been the result of their favourable tax and accounting treatment. Share options represent a relatively unique form of deferred compensation, where the recipient has substantial discretion in determining when to realise taxable income. Furthermore, in the past the cost of share options has not generally been expensed in a company's accounts, so that stock option compensation has essentially been free from an accounting perspective. This benefit has, however, largely disappeared as accounting standards now generally require companies to recognise the cost of granting stock options. The tax and accounting treatment of share options is dealt with in more detail in Chapter 6.

Stock options reward only stock price appreciation and not total shareholder returns, as dividends on the underlying shares are not payable until the options have been exercised. Some plans offer dividend equivalents – cash bonuses equal to the dividends which would have been paid on the underlying stock. The incentive effect of stock options does not, however,

Stock options give the right to buy shares at an agreed price in the future and typically expire after ten years.

mimic actual share ownership for a number of reasons. The value of an option increases with both stock price volatility and the length of time before expiry. Executives holding options may be encouraged to make risky investment decisions; an option is, after all, in effect a one-way bet. Conversely, 'underwater' options, where the strike price is higher than the current share price because the share price has fallen, have little or no incentive effect; indeed executives holding underwater options often describe them as a powerful disincentive. Option repricing is the practice of reducing the exercise price of underwater options to the new market price of the shares, thereby reinstating the incentive effect. This practice has proved to be extremely unpopular with shareholder groups and is now used only occasionally.

Restricted stock

Largely because of the imperfect incentive effect, particularly during bear markets when share prices are generally falling, some companies have chosen to make awards of actual stock, rather than options over shares, as an alternative to or to complement stock options. In the US awards are typically in the form of restricted stock, which is restricted in the sense that dividend and transfer rights are only acquired over time and shares may be forfeited in certain circumstances. For example, the shares may be forgone if the executive leaves the company before the rights have fully vested, particularly if they are a bad leaver. Some companies require executives to acquire shares on their own account, but incentivise them to do this by providing free matching shares (these are sometimes called 'buy-one-get-one-free schemes'). The matching shares may be in the form of restricted stock, so that the executive only acquires full ownership rights in these shares over a number of years, and not immediately.

Executives holding share options may be encouraged to make risky investment decisions; an option is, after all, in effect a one-way bet.

Performance shares

An alternative to restricted stock, more commonly used in the UK, are performance shares. These are promises to provide stock at a future date, subject to satisfactory corporate performance. Performance shares differ from restricted stock in that the shares are not actually issued at the time an award is made. The economic impact of the two types of arrangement is, however, essentially the same.

Deferred cash bonuses

Not all long-term incentive plans are share based. Some companies provide deferred cash bonuses, which might, for example, be declared at the end of an accounting year but paid some years later (three to five years is the norm) and only then if the executive is still employed by the company at the time the award finally crystallises. The deferred bonuses may earn a return linked to the company's financial performance during the period of deferral, for example return on capital employed (ROCE) or economic value added (EVA), which is basically profit after tax less the company's cost of capital. Some companies provide stock appreciation rights, which are deferred cash bonuses, the value of which is linked to the movement in the company's share price.

PENSIONS AND BENEFITS

The fourth component of a senior executive's total compensation is the benefits package. Executive benefits include company cars (particularly in the UK), health care (common across the world, but particularly significant in countries which do not have a universal health care system, such as the US and Australia), life insurance, disability cover and so on. But most significantly, especially in Western economies, executive benefits include pensions and other retirement benefits. Executive pensions and other benefits such as lump sums payable on ceasing work can be very substantial and sometimes controversial. Percy Barnevik, the charismatic CEO of Asea Brown Boveri (ABB), was criticised after it was discovered that he had drawn CHF148 million (Swiss francs) in retirement benefits between 1996, when he retired from ABB, and 2002. He subsequently agreed to repay CHF90 million. Even the iconic Jack Welch of GE attracted adverse publicity when he was awarded special retirement benefits worth $2.5 million per year in addition to an annual pension of $9 million, compared with final-year earnings of $16 million. He too agreed to make good the value of the special benefits.

Lucian Bebchuk and Robert J. Jackson of Harvard Law School have drawn attention to the fact that the pensions of American senior executives are sometimes enormous; they call them stealth compensation because of the limited disclosure of retirement benefits currently required under US generally accepted accounting principles.[2] But they also point out that there are huge variations between companies in the value of pension awards, and hence in the cost to shareholders.

Senior executives in Western companies are typically provided with pensions on a defined-benefit basis, where payouts are related to an individual's final salary and years of service. This continues to be the case even though many companies are switching their all-employee pension plans onto a defined contribution basis, where amounts paid in by the company are predetermined, not payments to retired employees; in other words it is a company's inputs, not outputs, which are fixed, and investment risk is borne by the individual. Because most countries place restrictions on tax-approved retirement benefits, companies often provide top-up pension plans – for example supplemental executive retirement plans (SERPs) in the US and funded unapproved retirement benefits schemes (FURBSs) in the UK. Top-up pensions may be funded by being held off-balance sheet, for example in a separate trust, or unfunded, in which case they appear as provisions on the company's balance sheet and are at risk like all other creditors in the event of

---

2   Bebchuk, L. and Jackson, R.J. (2005), *Putting Executive Pensions on the Radar Screen*, John M. Olin Discussion Paper Series, No. 507, Harvard Law School.

the company's insolvency. Supplemental executive pension arrangements are often very expensive for the companies which provide them, given the limits on the amounts which can be contributed without losing tax advantages.

TOTAL REWARD

Figure 3 is a model of how the various components of total reward described so far fit together.

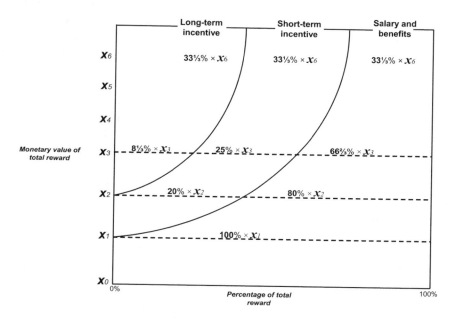

Figure 3 Total reward model for senior executives

The base level of income to be delivered as fixed salary and benefits is represented by x_1. Up to this point a fixed and certain income is required to maintain the executive's desired standard of living, to provide cash flow and collateral for loans. To place any part of total compensation at risk up to this level would be a positive disincentive to the recipient. Between x_1 and x_2 an annual bonus or short-term incentive is introduced, putting some income at risk and incentivising short-term performance. At x_2 a long-term incentive is added, increasing the amount of income at risk and providing motivation to sustain performance over a longer period (typically thought of in terms of three to five years). The proportion of total pay represented by the long-term incentive is initially relatively modest (8⅓% at x_3 in this example, compared with an annual bonus of 25% of total compensation and fixed salary of 66⅔%). As total reward increases the proportions change: the annual bonus and long-term incentive increase as a proportion of total compensation, and fixed salary declines. At x_6 we reach what is arguably the optimum point: total reward is split equally between fixed salary, annual bonuses and long-term incentives.

As total reward increases, the proportions change: the annual bonus and long-term incentives increase as a proportion of total compensation.

COMPENSATION, BENEFITS AND INCENTIVES

Salaries are, in effect, the basic reward for attending to duties. Bonuses are awarded for meeting short-term performance targets. Long-term incentives are the reward for achieving strategic objectives over a longer period, in particular for building sustainable shareholder value. There is a strong prima facie case for saying that these three elements should be kept in balance.

Note that the value of the long-term incentive shown here is the present value of the future expected payment added in the year. Actual cash payments to executives, taken on a year-by-year basis, may be 'lumpy' as they will depend on the maturing of long-term incentive awards such as the date that share options are exercised. This can distort the way that a senior executive's employment income is reported: an unusually high level of reward in a particular year may, for example, be because of a one-off exercise of share options.

In the same way, the value of the benefits package includes the present value of future additional retirement benefits added during the year. This is easy to calculate in the case of a defined-contribution plan, and more difficult (but not impossible) where executive pensions are provided on a defined-benefits basis.

TERMINATION PAYMENTS

There is one final, often contentious, element of executive pay which we must touch upon; termination payments. Executives whose employment ceases before their normal retirement age typically receive a lump sum payment, particularly if the cessation of employment has been initiated by the employer. The payment is normally linked to the unexpired element of the executive's contract. There may also be an ex gratia element. If the executive is old enough, pension payments may be brought forward. The employment contracts of some top managers actually specify what payments should be made if an executive is asked to leave, known as 'golden parachute' clauses. In the US golden parachutes are commonly linked to company takeovers, and special tax rules apply.

Termination payments are contentious because they are often large and by definition are made for non-performance.

Termination payments are contentious because they are often large and by definition are made not for performing a contract but for non-performance. In the UK they are sometimes pejoratively referred to as 'payments for failure': it is executives who fail to perform satisfactorily who are asked to leave, not successful ones. The principle of pay for performance is thereby turned on its head. On the other hand all employees, whatever their level of seniority, are entitled to some protection against the unfair actions of employers, including breach of contract.

CHAPTER 3

Economic Models

WHY THE MARKET DOESN'T WORK

'My remuneration', said the CEO of a large UK quoted company in response to a question at his company's annual general meeting, 'is determined by market forces. There is really nothing more to say on the matter.' Self-justification on the subject of pay is never easy, especially when faced with a group of hostile shareholders. Even so, the CEO's response was a weak one. Worse, it showed a fundamental misunderstanding of microeconomics.

According to classical microeconomic theory, a perfect market requires many buyers and sellers, homogeneous products (or at least good substitutes), free market entry and exit, plentiful information and little economic friction (any factors that inhibit the free operation of the market). The trouble with the market for senior executives is that practically none of these conditions hold good. At any one time only a few top jobs may be open, and only a limited number of suitable candidates may be available. No two senior executives are the same and information about them is far from perfect. Information about prices (what executives are paid) is far from perfect too, despite the best endeavours of governments and regulators over the past ten years. Finally, all sorts of legal, tax and accounting factors impact on the way senior executives are paid and the types of contracts companies choose to enter into with them. So the theory of supply and demand from classical microeconomics has only a limited amount to say that is helpful about the question of executive pay.

At any one time, only a few top jobs may be open and only a limited number of suitable candidates may be available.

What the CEO probably meant when he talked about market forces was that others who occupied similar positions were paid more. He was probably particularly concerned by the fact that, even though his company had significant business operations in the US, as the CEO of a UK-based company he was paid less than many of his North American counterparts.

AGENCY THEORY

Economists have typically sought to explain executive pay in terms of 'agency theory'. In public companies the executives, who run the business, are different people from the shareholders, who own it. The executives (agents) are meant to run the business primarily for the benefit of shareholders (principals). In practice conflicts of interest arise. This is true even if we apply the enlightened value maximisation assumption referred to in the previous chapter, as opposed to the more traditional theory of shareholder value maximisation. Even if executives, as stakeholders, also have a legitimate interest in the residual profits of a company, their interest is not the same as that of shareholders.

Summary: Agency theory proposes that the interests of the executives who run the business differ from those of the shareholders who own it; incentive contracts and careful monitoring are therefore necessary.

There are various areas of difference. Executives receive their reward (salary, bonuses, stock options and so on) in a different way from shareholders (dividends and capital gains). As a consequence, they might seek to pay themselves excessive salaries and benefits. They may retain profits rather than paying out dividends to reduce the company's financial risk. Executives and shareholders have different risk profiles. Executives may not wish to take risks with the company's assets that shareholders, with the advantage of diversification, might be prepared to take; if the company fails the shareholders have lost only a part of their investment portfolios, but the executives stand to lose their livelihoods. Conversely some executives might take exceptional and inappropriate risks, as their own money is not at stake. The time horizon of many executives is shorter than that of many shareholders, who are often in for the long term. This might result in an unwillingness to invest in long-term projects. A Booz Allen Hamilton report describes CEOs as 'The World's Most Prominent Temp Workers' on the basis that the average tenure of a CEO in the US and Europe is now less than five years.[1] If you are a CEO you don't have long to prove yourself!

According to agency theory, shareholders can exercise control or influence the behaviours of executives in two ways:

- They must design incentive contracts which attempt to align the interests of shareholders and executives by rewarding executives when value is created for the firm and by not rewarding them, other than through basic salary and benefits, when it is not;
- They must monitor the actions of executives carefully, ensuring that rigorous procedures are in place to approve all major decisions as well as any decisions where conflicts of interest are likely to arise.

We will deal with the second of these control mechanisms, corporate governance, later in the book. Let's begin with incentive contracts.

---

1   Lucier, C., Schuyt, R. and Tse, E. (2005), *The World's Most Prominent Temp Workers*, Booz Allen Hamilton annual study of CEO succession.

Principal–agent model

Kevin Murphy describes how in a typical principal–agent model executives are assumed to take actions to produce value for the firm, in return receiving tangible and intangible benefits (utility in the language of economists) and, specifically, financial compensation. This financial compensation depends on actions producing shareholder value as well as other observable features, which do not, and are strictly irrelevant, but still form part of the contract.[2] The executives' utility function and the way in which their actions are linked to outputs are assumed to be common ground, recognised and understood by both executives and shareholders alike. However, only the executives are necessarily aware of the actions taken: the shareholders may know what actions they want the executives to take but cannot always directly observe what happens in practice.

The optimal contract maximises the shareholders' objective (value created for the firm less financial compensation awarded to the executives) subject to two constraints:

- an incentive compatibility constraint (the executives' objective of maximising their utility may not fully align with the principals' objective of maximising shareholder value);
- a participation constraint (the expected utility resulting from the contract must at a minimum exceed the executives' minimum required utility).

An executive's own wealth creation objective is explicitly tied to the shareholder value objective if he also holds stock in the company.

The traditional principal–agent model yields several important and practical insights which may help to understand existing contracts and in designing better ones.

- An executive's own wealth creation objective is explicitly tied to the shareholder value objective if he or she also holds stock in the company. Their objectives can also be aligned by giving executives equity-based long-term incentive plans (stock options, restricted stock and so on). In addition, executive wealth is implicitly tied to shareholder value through bonuses linked to accounting measures, reflecting the correlation between accounting returns and stock price performance, as well as through year-by-year adjustment to base salaries, target bonuses, stock option grants and so forth.
- Incentives for executives are best linked to outcomes (for example, an increase in stock values) rather than inputs (the executives' behaviours and actions). This is because of the problem (referred to by economists as a moral hazard problem) which arises because shareholders cannot observe all the executives' actions.
- The model highlights the trade-off between risks and incentives. Wealth creation incentives are strongest for executives with an appetite to take risks, and weaker for risk-averse executives. This touches upon another problem. Shareholders, who are able to spread their risk by diversifying

2   Murphy, K.J. (1999), Op. Cit.

ECONOMIC
MODELS

their portfolios, may have a greater appetite for risk than executives, who often have much of their wealth, as well as their employment, tied up in their companies. The executives' attitude to risk is likely to be dependent up to a point on the extent of their wealth: the wealthier they are, the greater their appetite for risk.

- The model explains why incentives should not only be construed in financial terms, but should recognise that executives' wish to maximise their utility generally. This insight has been taken up in practice by the total reward school of executive reward policy design.

Principal–agent model for executive compensation

Agency theory has been the subject of a great deal of highly complex mathematical analysis. For the more mathematically minded, the essential features of the principal–agent model are shown here in mathematical notation.

Actions of executives	$= a$
Value produced for the firm	$= v(a)$
Executives' utility function	$= u(a)$

Executives' financial compensation function $= c\{v(a), o\}$, where 'c' depends on actions producing shareholder value, '$v(a)$', as well as other observable features, 'o' which do not.

Executives' optimal contract	$= c^*\{v(a),o\}$
Shareholders' value maximisation objective	$= v(a) - c$

Two constraints:

1. Incentive compatibility: $u(a)$ must align with $v(a) - c$
2. Participation constraint: $v(a)$ must be greater than $u(a)$

From these initial premises complex mathematical models have been developed. They are intended, among other things, to explain the necessary characteristics of an optimum incentive contract given a particular set of facts.

After Murphy (1999)

Shortcomings of agency theory

However, the simplified principal–agent model set out above also illustrates some of the weaknesses of agency theory. According to classical agency theory, the principal knows what actions the agent should take in order to maximise value for the principal. Yet the reason shareholders trust their money to self-interested executives is often because of the professional managers' superior skills, knowledge and information, which allow them to

The reason shareholders trust their money to self-interested executives is often because of the professional managers' superior skills, knowledge and information.

make better investment decisions. This limitation is compensated for to some extent by focusing incentives on outcomes not inputs.

While incentive contracts are typically linear (by making rewards under long-term incentive plans commensurate with increases in stock price), the actual relationship between pay and stock price performance may be convex or concave, and need not be positive throughout its entire range. For example, in some cases very high returns may only be obtainable by taking very high risk ('bet the business') actions which may be beyond the limits of a typical shareholder's range of acceptable risks. In these circumstances, an optimal incentive contract should be designed to discourage returns above a certain level if linked inextricably with very high risk.

As has been shown, the function which connects executive utility with shareholder value may be fairly complex, and involve multiple metrics. Yet a good reason for not using all possible measures is that the resulting system may end up being too complicated for anyone to understand. In that case it cannot motivate effectively. This possibility would seem to limit the potential effectiveness of schemes that call for large numbers of measures, including certain variants of the balanced scorecard system. An important principle in designing reward plans is that they must be capable of being understood (by executives) as well as explained (to shareholders).

Allocation problems

Agency theory does not deal particularly well with allocation problems. Although the model summarised above demonstrates a link between the performance of a group of executives and shareholder value, it does not explain how the performance of individual executives contributes to overall group performance. Conflicts of interest may exist: a business-unit leader whose incentive is linked to business-unit performance may take actions which are detrimental to the overall performance of the company. Cooperation between executives may be hard to measure. Free-riding may be possible, and some imbalance of effort is probably inevitable. And there will often be a conflict between measures intended to maximise performance in the short term, and investments necessary to build future business.

We can see that agency theory, far more than classical microeconomics, provides helpful insights into the executive pay question. These insights are both descriptive, helping to explain why things are the way they are, and normative, suggesting ways in which executives' contracts might be designed. In particular, agency theory explains the importance of having carefully structured incentives contracts, linking the interests of shareholders and executives. But this is easier to do in theory than in practice. Effective incentive contracts which really do cause executives to look to the interests of shareholders are notoriously difficult to construct. What other economic theories are there that help to answer the executive pay question? In particular, why is it that executive pay arrangements so often give sub-optimal

Effective incentive contracts which really do cause executives to look to the interests of shareholders are notoriously difficult to construct.

ECONOMIC MODELS

results? To answer these questions let us turn to systems thinking and game theory.

SYSTEMS THINKING

Some clues can be found in the field of systems thinking, and in particular how positive and negative feedback processes shape system dynamics. Systems characterised by the preponderance of positive (or reinforcing) feedback, where more leads to more and less to less, are inherently unstable. Positive feedback is important in explaining escalating patterns of systems change. Systems characterised by an abundance of negative (or balancing) feedback are, on the other hand, inherently stable: a change in a variable initiates a counteracting force, leading to a change in the opposite direction and eventually to renewed equilibrium.

Pay benchmarking, as described in Chapter 2, which is often a core part of the work performed by compensation consultants for remuneration committees, is a process based substantially on positive feedback. If a benchmarking exercise demonstrates that the executives of company A are paid on average less than the executives of comparator companies B, C and D, then company A's remuneration committee may decide it has good reasons for increasing the pay of its executives. If subsequently company A is included in a pay benchmarking exercise carried out on behalf of company B or C, then this may in turn create a reason for the remuneration committee of those companies to increase the pay of their executives; and so the spiral continues. However, the converse is not true: if a benchmarking process shows that company A's executives are on average paid favourably in comparison with B and C, then their remuneration will not be reduced; indeed, for contract and employment law reasons, it may be difficult to do this.

One way of looking at the increasing emphasis on strong corporate governance processes in recent years is that corporate governance is a way of incorporating checks, balances and controls into a system which would otherwise be inherently unstable. To be effective corporate governance should involve negative feedback processes to counteract the preponderance of positive feedback. These processes should require justification for pay increases which looks beyond mere benchmarking. Additional constraints should be built in and as far as possible compensation (at least the incentive pay component) should be capable of going down as well as up.

But systems thinking also explains why disclosing the pay of individual executives, as happens in the UK in the case of company directors, may actually be positively unhelpful. Like benchmarking, disclosure of individual pay packages can start an upwards spiral (the result of a positive feedback loop) as executives compare their earnings and the less well remunerated use data about other people's pay to argue for an increase.

There is a trade-off here: full disclosure helps to eliminate the moral hazard problem arising out of the principal–agent relationship by bringing to light egregious remuneration practices. But it may do so at the expense of triggering or perpetuating a cycle of accelerating pay – an interesting example of the application of the law of unintended consequences!

GAME THEORY

The origins of game theory lie in work performed in the 1940s and 1950s in the US by a number of highly gifted mathematicians, two of the most famous being John von Neumann and John Nash. (John Nash's story has been immortalised in the film *A Beautiful Mind*, based on the book by Sylvia Nasar.[3]) This group of mathematicians worked for various academic and governmental organisations against the background of the Cold War, and much of their early work was designed to help analyse and solve military conflicts.

Two criminals are arrested. The police offer each a Faustian bargain: testify against the other and go free.

Von Neumann saw other applications for game theory. In particular he felt the developing methodologies would be valuable in the field of economics. Accordingly, he teamed up with a Princeton economist, Osker Morgenstern, to expand this line of thinking. In 1944 they published their findings in a book called *Theory of Games and Economic Behaviour*, which was to become a pioneering work in both economics and game theory. As well as warfare, diplomacy and economics, game theory has subsequently been applied in many other fields of human endeavour, including sport, sociology and even biology. In business, game theory has been used successfully to analyse pricing strategies, contract negotiations and auctions, among other things.

Prisoner's dilemma

William Poundstone, in his book *Prisoner's Dilemma*, describes game theory's most famous puzzle like this.[4] Suppose that two criminals are arrested and imprisoned, with no means of conferring with each other. The police recognise that they do not have enough evidence to convict the pair on the principal charge, but would expect to get both sentenced to a year in prison on a lesser count. Simultaneously, they offer each prisoner a Faustian bargain. They tell each one that if he testifies against his partner in the crime he will go free, while his partner will get five years in prison on the main charge. If both testify against each other, they will both serve two years in jail. Both know that they are being offered the same deal, but they will not learn what the other has decided until they have made their decisions. The two prisoners, who are interested only in their own welfare, rationalise the situation like this. The best result is obtained by testifying against their partner, as long as the other prisoner does not do likewise. But even if he does, the result – a two-year jail sentence – is still better than the worst case scenario – a five-year

---

3   Nasar, S. (1998), *A Beautiful Mind*, Faber and Faber, London.

4   Poundstone, W. (1992), *Prisoner's Dilemma*, Doubleday, New York.

ECONOMIC MODELS

sentence. So the rational response for the two prisoners is to testify against each other, even though a better result for both in aggregate terms might have been obtained by remaining silent.

In diagram form, the range of outcomes is as shown in Figure 4. Pay-offs, the utility to each player of each possible outcome, are shown by the numbers in brackets. The first number is the pay-off for Prisoner A. The second number is the pay-off for Prisoner B. In this case the numbers are negative, as they represent the period of years to be spent in jail. Scenario 4, the least worst option or 'maximin', is chosen by the two prisoners even though the result is worse – in aggregate and individually – than in Scenario 1.

| | Prisoner B | |
	Remain silent	Testify
Remain silent	Scenario 1 (-1, -1)	Scenario 3 (-5, 0)
Testify	Scenario 2 (0, -5)	Scenario 4 (-2,-2)

Where:

   0 = strong preference for (go free)
  -1 = marginal preference for (one-year sentence)
  -2 = marginal preference against (two-year sentence)
  -5 = very strong preference against (five-year sentence)

Figure 4 The prisoner's dilemma

Why do top-rank professional sportsmen earn more in a week than the majority of similar professionals in a year?

WINNER-TAKES-ALL PHENOMENON

It is a curious feature of the free market that in many trades, professions and occupations the few at the top often earn many times more than the average; in statistical terms the arithmetic mean (the total of everyone's earnings divided by the number of people in the relevant category) is significantly higher than the median (the mid-point in terms of ranking). This phenomenon, which two American economists have called 'winner-takes-all',[5] is most noticeable in professional sport. Why do top-rank professional footballers, basketball or baseball players earn more in a week than the majority of similar professionals earn in a year? If all the players of a particular sport earned modest amounts, then the coach of one team might reason as follows: if he was able to pay well above the odds then he would be able to recruit the best players, win lots of trophies, attract large crowds and secure the best sponsorship deals. The trouble is that other coaches will reason in the same way, so that paying high wages becomes a dominant strategy. This is another example of the prisoner's dilemma where the inevitable logic of the situation leads to a position which is sub-optimal for every team; no team wants to be left with the least able players, thereby running the risk of failure on the field or court with all its consequential financial implications. So everybody decides to pay over the odds!

Some sports governing bodies, particularly in the US, have realised this and have tried to place caps on players earnings or on the total amounts that teams can spend on wages. Player's unions of course resist this in any way they can!

In the same way, companies face a prisoner's dilemma when it comes to chief executive officers' pay. To demonstrate this let us assume that all CEOs are paid broadly equal amounts, with only marginal variations in pay justifiable by reference to job size, industry, specialist expertise and so on. Assume also that in the available population of CEOs, 20% are superior to the others and would, if they worked for your company, increase the value of the firm by more than the average. Conversely, 10% are inferior to the others and would, if you employed them, potentially reduce the firm's value.

If all companies offered modest remuneration, then it would be in the interests of an individual company to defect and pay over the odds.

If all companies offered modest remuneration, then it would be in the interests of an individual company to defect and pay over the odds. By doing so they might attract top talent and (potentially) be more successful than their competitors. Conversely, a company would not want to find itself in the position of paying significantly below average. To do so might mean it could only attract inferior chief executives. No one will congratulate a company's remuneration committee for its financial prudence if the result is a second-rate management team. Thus offering higher salaries is the dominant strategy, even though by doing so companies will generally be no better off than if they all paid modest salaries. On the other hand this is better than risking being in the bottom 10%.

This is, incidentally, strangely reminiscent of the words of Al Dunlop ('Chainsaw Al'), former CEO of Sunbeam Corporation, who is reported to have once said: 'The best bargain is an expensive CEO; you cannot overpay a good CEO and you can't underpay a bad one.' He clearly did not understand game theory!

---

5   Frank, R.H. and Cook, P.J. (1985), *The Winner-Takes-All Society: How More and More Americans Compete for Ever Fewer and Bigger Prizes, Encouraging Economic Waste, Income Inequality, and an Impoverished Cultural Life*, Free Press, New York.

ECONOMIC
MODELS

REMUNERATION COMMITTEE'S DILEMMA

We can represent the problem which remuneration committees face (let us call it the 'remuneration committee's dilemma') with the same kind of pay-off table as we used for the prisoner's dilemma (see Figure 5).

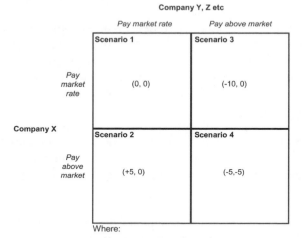

Company Y, Z etc

Company X	Pay market rate	Pay above market
Pay market rate	**Scenario 1** (0, 0)	**Scenario 3** (-10, 0)
Pay above market	**Scenario 2** (+5, 0)	**Scenario 4** (-5,-5)

Where:

+5 = strong preference for (get top performer)

0 = marginal preference for (get satisfactory performer at market rate)

-5 = marginal preference against (get satisfactory performer at above market rate)

-10 = very strong preference against (get inferior performer)

Scenario 4 is the dominant strategy; everyone pays over the odds.

Figure 5 Remuneration committee's dilemma

Scenario 1 is the neutral option; every company pays the market rate and accepts the quality of chief executive they get. In Scenario 2, Company X defects and pays over the odds in the hope of getting a top performer who will materially influence the value of the company. In Scenario 3, Company X is left paying the market rate while everyone else pays over the odds, thereby running the risk of hiring inferior talent who will negatively impact on the company's net worth. Scenario 4 is the dominant strategy; everyone pays over the odds, but in doing so neither increases nor reduces the likelihood that they will recruit superior talent.

Tournament models

An alternative, complementary explanation of the 'winner-takes-all' phenomenon is given by tournament theory. Tournament models propose that executive pay is a function of job level and promotion prospects, and the result of a series of 'tournaments' which take place as executives progress through the corporate hierarchy. For junior executives, promotion prospects are good: there are a good number of promotion opportunities available relative to the number of promotion candidates. As a consequence pay increases linked to promotion need only be modest to generate an adequate incentive effect: future expected pay (itself a function of the size of the promotion pay increase and the probability of promotion) is high simply because of the number of promotion opportunities available. At more senior levels, however, promotion opportunities decrease: a smaller number of candidates is required to fill the jobs available. Consequentially, higher promotion pay rises are required to maintain future expected pay at a sufficiently high level to generate an adequate incentive effect. At the highest rung of the corporate ladder, the probability of promotion to CEO is so small that a very high relative rate of pay is required to maintain an adequate incentive effect for senior executives operating just below CEO level.

A simple model illustrates this. Imagine a company with five executive-level job grades, from manager to CEO, where starting pay for executives is £75000 and individuals expect a promotion pay increase of at least 7.5% on current levels if promotion is to be perceived to be worthwhile. According to tournament theory the pay build-up would be as set out in Table 1.

Tournament theory emphasises that a peron's job and job changes are key drivers of executive pay, rather than competencies, experience and knowledge.

Table 1 Tournament model of executive pay

Level	Number of Executives	Probability of Promotion (%)	Expected Pay (£)	Percentage Increase on Promotion
1	500	40%	£75000	–
2	200	25%	£89065	18.75%
3	50	20%	£115785	30.00%
4	10	10%	£159205	37.50%
5	1	–	£278610	75.00%

The probability of promotion from level 1 to level 2 is 40% (200/500 × 100). The increase in pay necessary to give the expectation of a 7.5% pay increase is 7.5%/40% or 18.75%. The probability of promotion from level 2 to level 3 is 25% (50/200 × 100), so that the increase in pay necessary to give an expected pay rise of 7.5% is 7.5%/25% or 30%, and so on. Note that the probability of a level 1 executive becoming chief executive is the product of all the percentages in column 3, that is 40% × 25% × 20% × 10%, or 0.2%.

If on top of this you add one further complication, the possibility that the CEO's role is equally likely to be filled by an external candidate as an internal candidate, then the expected pay for the CEO increases to £398015,[6] a 150% increase over pay at executive level 4.

The key insights given by tournament theory are these. Tournament theory emphasises that a person's job and changes in job are key drivers of executive pay, rather than their competencies, experience and knowledge (their 'human

---

6   £159205 + (7.5%/5.0% × £159205) = £398015

capital' to use the language of labour economics once again). Pay growth over time is not smooth, but has kinks because of the effect of pay rises occurring on promotion. The incentive effect of tournaments is tied directly to the size of the pay differentials between ranks or job levels. Effort is linked to the size of the differential and the probability of success.

Pay growth is larger at higher job levels than at lower grades because the number of opportunities for future promotion is smaller and the probability of promotion is accordingly less. To maintain the expected value of promotion at a sufficiently high level there must be an increase in the pay-off to offset the reduction in probability of promotion. In other words, the relationship between job level and pay is convex (see Figure 6).

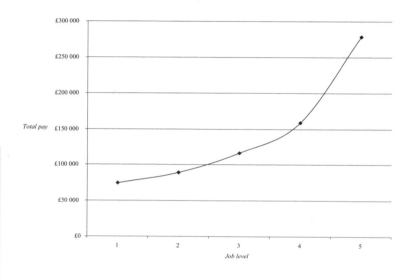

Figure 6 Tournament model of executive pay

Tournament theory does not require the marginal product of an individual to be greater than or equal to the marginal pay at any given level. Indeed, executives at the highest job levels do not need to be worth the extra pay for the overall incentive effect of the pay scheme to be efficient in economic terms. This is because the efficiency properties are a result of the incentive effect that large pay rises at higher job levels may have on employees who are lower down in the hierarchy. This might explain why CEOs are sometimes thought not to be worth the additional pay which they receive!

LIMITS OF ECONOMIC ANALYSIS

While economic analysis provides some important insights into the determinants of executive reward, economists tend to deal in averages, aggregate behaviours and in the consequences of different behaviours. As we shall see in the next chapter, psychologists tend to be more interested in psychological processes at an individual level and in what drives different behaviours. Economists generally view monetary reward as an end in itself, whereas psychologists are interested in the underlying cognitive processes which may be translated into monetary rewards. In psychological terms, money may be a way of calibrating value or worth, rather than a first-order measure. Neither approach is right or wrong; a true explanation of the facts almost certainly comes from some combination of both perspectives.

In this chapter we have learnt about the limitations of markets and the price mechanism in helping to explain senior executive pay and how agency theory gives us the idea of the incentive contract as a way of aligning the interests of executives and shareholders. We have been introduced to the idea that governance processes also have an important part to play in regulating the contract between principals (shareholders) and agents (executives). Chapter 5 will deal with this in more detail. We have observed a phenomenon ('winner-takes-all') resulting in a paradox which I have called the 'remuneration committee's dilemma', as well as a possible solution in tournament theory. We have also discovered some of the practical limitations of economic theory as a means of explaining executive compensation. We must now leave the realms of economics and see what light psychology, sociology and organisational behaviour can shed on the executive pay question.

Economists view monetary reward as an end in itself; psychologists say it is a way of calibrating value or worth.

CHAPTER 4

Psychology, Sociology and Organisational Behaviour

The ultimatum game illustrates the limits of economic analysis built around the assumption of rational economic man.

ULTIMATUM GAME

James Surowiecki, a columnist for *The New Yorker* magazine, has suggested that some clues to the executive pay question might be found in behavioural game theory, in particular an experiment called the 'ultimatum game'.[1] The rules of this game are simple. An experimenter brings two people together. They can share information but are otherwise anonymous to each other. Person A is given £100 and is told she can split this in any way she likes with Person B. Person B can accept the offer or, if he prefers, reject it. If B accepts the offer then A and B both get their money. But if B rejects the offer then, and here's the rub, neither B nor A gets to keep the money.

If B was a rational economic man, then he would accept even a modest offer, as he will inevitably be better off with something rather than nothing. A's position is strictly irrelevant; B has not met her before and will not see her again. Yet in practice modest offers are typically refused. The responder would rather have nothing than let the proposer walk away with more than her fair share. The most common offers in the ultimatum game, in fact, are between £40 and £50. Some proposers even offer more than 50% of the sum available, recognising that some responders need to feel that they are going to get more than their fair share as an inducement to accept the deal.

The ultimatum game illustrates a number of things:

*   It shows the limits of economic analysis built around the assumption of rational economic man;

---

1   Surowiecki, J. (2004), *The Wisdom of Crowds: Why the Many are Smarter than the Few and How Collective Wisdom Shapes Business, Economies, Societies and Nations*, Little, Brown, London.

- It shows the significance of fairness and trust: the responder needs to feel that he is being treated fairly; otherwise he is prepared to make a financial sacrifice and give up his share of the £100 to make a point to the offeror by imposing a financial penalty upon her.

Extrinsic motivation is gained by satisfying an external need, intrinsic motivation by undertaking a task to satisfy an intrinsic need.

Culture is also relevant. In the US, lower offers are more frequently made and more frequently accepted. In Japan, proposers will generally offer 50% of the money which is available. Japanese responders would be surprised if they did not. Let us explore these two ideas further, first by looking at some of the psychological theories of motivation, and second by looking at the impact of culture.

TRADITIONAL THEORIES OF MOTIVATION

Although agency theory assumes that incentives have an impact on motivation and effort, economists have generally neglected the psychological factors affecting senior executive compensation. Organisational psychologists on the other hand have examined the concepts of motivation and effort for many years. However, they have done so largely in an industrial context: the traditional theories typically look at the motivation of the wider workforce in a factory or warehouse situation, rather than at senior executives.

Research by psychologists has distinguished between intrinsic and extrinsic motivational factors. Extrinsic motivation is gained by satisfying external needs, and is therefore stimulated by (among other things) monetary incentives. Agency theorists rely exclusively on extrinsic motivation to assess the amount of effort an agent is expected to expend. In this way they neglect the potential impact of intrinsic motivation on the incentive contract. Intrinsic motivation means that under certain conditions employees are prepared to undertake a task for its own sake or for the satisfaction of some other kind of intrinsic need; some tasks will therefore be performed without monetary payment.

Maslow's hierarchy of needs

The intrinsic motivation theories derive their fundamental ideas from some general assumptions about human needs, on the lines originally advocated by Abraham Maslow in 1954.[2] Maslow categorised basic human needs into a hierarchy, traditionally represented in the form of a triangle (see Figure 7).

Maslow suggests that needs are only motivators when unsatisfied. He says that these needs function, roughly, in an order of priority. The lower order needs (physiological and safety) are dominant until satisfied, whereupon the higher-order needs come into operation.

---

2   Maslow, A.H. (1954), *Motivation and Personality*, Harper & Row, New York.

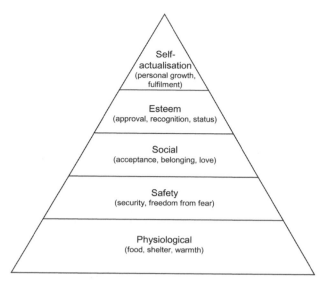

Figure 7   Maslow's hierarchy of needs

McGregor's Theory X and Theory Y

In the 1960s Douglas McGregor set out two propositions – Theory X and Theory Y.[3] Under Theory X the assumption is that people are basically lazy; they work as little as possible. They lack ambition, dislike responsibility and are resistant to change. The implications for management are that people must be persuaded, rewarded, punished, directed and controlled. Management is responsible for organising the elements of productive enterprise. Under Theory Y, people are inherently motivated, have the potential for development, the capacity to assume responsibility and the readiness to direct behaviour towards organisational goals. Management is responsible for organising the elements of productive enterprise in the interest of economic ends, but its essential task is to arrange the conditions and methods of operation so that people can achieve their goals best by directing their own efforts towards organisational objectives.

Frederick Herzberg – motivation and hygiene factors

Frederick Herzberg maintained that in any work situation you can distinguish between the factors that dissatisfy and those that motivate.[4] The interesting thing is that they are not opposites; dealing with the dissatisfying factors does not turn them into satisfying factors. In general, the dissatisfying factors are things to do with conditions of work – company policy and administration, supervision, salary, interpersonal relations and physical working conditions. Herzberg called these the 'hygiene' or 'maintenance factors'. They are the necessary conditions of successful motivation. The satisfiers are achievement,

Herzberg maintained that in any work situation you can distinguish between the factors that dissatisfy and those that motivate.

---

3   McGregor, D.M. (1960), *The Human Side of Enterprise*, McGraw-Hill, New York.

4   Herzberg, F. (1966), *Work and the Nature of Man*, World Publishing Company, Cleveland.

PSYCHOLOGY,
SOCIOLOGY AND
ORGANISATIONAL
BEHAVIOUR

recognition, work itself, responsibility and advancement. These he called 'motivators'.

Aldefer's ERG model

Clayton Aldefer simplified Maslow's needs down to three categories – the need for existence, the need to relate to others and the need for personal growth.[5] This is known as the ERG model after the three categories – existence, relatedness and growth. Like Marlow's model, ERG theory is hierarchical; existence needs motivate at a more fundamental level than relatedness needs, which in turn come before growth needs. However, unlike Maslow, Aldefer recognised that categories overlap. There are circumstances when a lower-order need is not fully satisfied before a higher-order need becomes a factor influencing behaviour; the 'starving artist' scenario. Aldefer is also at pains to point out that needs are different for different types of people and that individuals may regress to more basic needs if higher order needs are frustrated. This flexibility allows ERG theory to account for a wider range of observed behaviour than Maslow's original model.

Victor Vroom – expectation theory

Maslow, McGregor, Herzberg and Aldefer all look at motivation in terms of needs, and their theories are therefore known as 'needs-based' theories. Victor Vroom on the other hand looks at motivation in terms of expectations.[6] He calls the preference an individual has for a particular outcome 'valence'. A person may seek or avoid certain outcomes, or may be ambivalent about them, so valence can be positive, negative or neutral. Vroom describes an individual's expectations that particular behaviour will lead to a certain outcome as subjective probability. It is subjective because people have different views about the relationship between particular behaviours and outcomes. Expectation or subjective probability can have values between 0 (no likelihood that a particular behaviour will lead to a particular outcome) and 1 (absolute certainty that it will). Strength of motivation thus depends on both valence and expectation and can be represented like this:

$$F = \sum(E \times V)$$

where:

F = motivation to behave in a certain way, otherwise known as 'force'

E = the expectation that a particular behaviour will lead to a certain outcome

V = the valence of that outcome.

ERG theory is hierarchical; existence needs motivate at a more fundamental level than relatedness needs, which in turn come before growth needs.

5   Aldefer, C.P. (1972), *Existence, Relatedness and Growth*, Free Press, New York.

6   Vroom, V.H. (1964), *Work and Motivation*, Wiley, New York.

The sigma sign ($\sum$) means 'the sum of all possible results'. It is incorporated into the formula because we must add up all the different possible outcomes from a certain set of behaviours in order to assess the strength of the motivational effect.

Charles Handy – the motivation calculus

In the 1970s Charles Handy attempted to combine needs theory and expectancy theory in what he calls the 'motivation calculus'.[7] This model states that each individual has a set of needs and a set of desired results. Results need to be evaluated in terms of how specific they are, how they are fixed, how feedback is obtained and so on. We decided how much E (effort, energy, excitement and so on) to expend by doing an (unconscious) calculation. The calculus operates within the limits of a contract, the psychological contract, which each individual has with the organisation they work for, the team they are part of and the manager they report to. The psychological contract is essentially a set of expectations. We have a set of results that we expect from the organisation, results that will satisfy certain of our needs in return for which we will apply some of our talents and expend some of our energy and effort.

Senior executives often have considerable esteem needs; for example, for status, recognition, approval and achievement.

You may think that the theories about motivation which have been described so far do little to explain what motivates very senior executives, and you would probably be entirely justified in thinking this. Two important insights do emerge, however.

- Senior executives have psychological needs too. We can probably generally assume that their basic needs are met, so that we are talking about what Maslow suggested are higher needs. Senior executives often have considerable esteem needs; for example for status, recognition, approval and achievement. Monetary rewards can be relevant to esteem needs, for the simple reason that they provide a method of calibration. Measuring the importance of a particular job by valuing the reward package which it commands allows comparisons to be made with seniors, juniors and most importantly with peers. At the beginning of Chapter 3 we saw how a CEO who felt he was being paid at below the market rate probably meant simply that he knew other people who were being paid more than he was.
- Senior executives are often very driven to achieve particular goals, which means that Vroom's expectancy theory and Handy's motivation calculus can be used to predict how individual executives will behave. This reinforces the idea of the incentive contract, with clearly stated objectives, which, if met, will benefit shareholders as much as their agents.

Crowding-out

Another approach, referred to rather confusingly as 'crowding theory', examines the relationship between intrinsic and extrinsic motivation,

---

7   Handy, C. (1976), *Understanding Organisations*, Penguin, London.

*Summary:
Crowding-out
theory examines
the relationship
between the
things we do
for their own
sake and the
things we do for
reward.*

between things that we do for their own sake and things which we do for reward.[8] Extrinsic rewards may support intrinsic motivation, providing a double incentive to act. This is called crowding-in. But extrinsic rewards might actually detract from intrinsic motivation; people may become distracted by rewards, particular if incentives are badly designed. In short, there may be noise in the system. This is known as crowding-out.

The labour supply curve represents the relationship between pay and effort. The economists' traditional view is that individuals will seek to maximise their own utility subject to the constraints imposed upon them, most importantly income and time. According to this way of thinking the labour supply curve is essentially straight, sloping from bottom left to top right (see Figure 8).

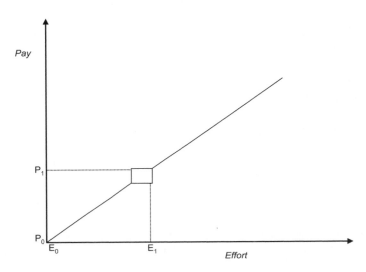

Figure 8 Simple labour supply curve

Individuals are motivated because increased effort leads to increased reward. Increasing rewards from P_0 to P_1 leads to an increase in effort from E_0 to E_1. 'Effort' incidentally in this context is used in a special sense. It means not only the energy expended, but also application of the intellect, strategic skills, execution capability, judgement and leadership that make up the skill-set of a competent corporate executive. To put it another way, it is a combination of energy and an individual's human capital.

According to the crowding-out principle, there comes a point when giving additional rewards may actually detract from intrinsic motivation, leading to a reduction in effort. People become temporarily blinded by what they earn. Money becomes more important than the intrinsic pleasure obtained from work, paradoxically leading in the short term to reduced motivation, given

---

8   See for example Frey, B.S. (1997), *Not Just For Money: An Economic Theory of Personal Motivation*, Edward Elgar Publishing, Cheltenham, UK.

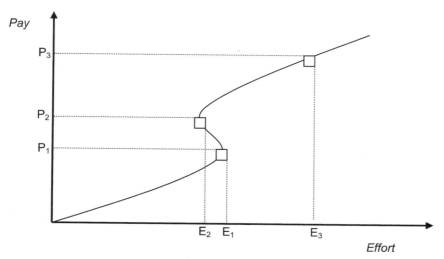

Figure 9 Labour supply curve with crowding-out

the other distractions. The theory goes on to say that at some point extrinsic reward takes over from intrinsic motivation, so that the supply curve reverts to the more normal upwards slope (Figure 9). In other words, the possibility of even greater rewards spurs people on once again.

Up to point P_1E_1 the increase in effort is commensurate to the increase in reward. Crowding-out then kicks in, as increasing reward distracts the individual and detracts from their intrinsic motivation. This noise in the system continues to P_2E_2, at which point the motivational effect of extrinsic reward is substituted for the effect of intrinsic motivation and the upwards gradient of the labour supply curve is restored.

A less extreme view of crowding theory, and one which provides the most likely hypothesis when it comes to executive compensation, is represented in Figure 10.

Over the first part of the labour supply curve, rewards positively reinforce intrinsic motivation, so that there is crowding-in. The labour supply curve is therefore initially convex. For a time the slope of the curve becomes flat as effort and reward increase proportionately (between P_1E_1 and P_2E_2 in the diagram). Thereafter the motivational effect of increased reward starts to diminish – a mild form of crowding-out if you like, although according to this hypothesis the trend is unlikely ever to become negative, as with true crowding-out. What this does mean is that increased effort is no longer commensurate with increased reward, so that the labour supply curve eventually becomes concave. To put it another way, there comes a point when it takes a very significant increase in reward to generate only a marginally noticeable increase in effort.

There comes a point when additional rewards may detract from intrinsic motivation, but then the possibility of even greater rewards spurs people on again.

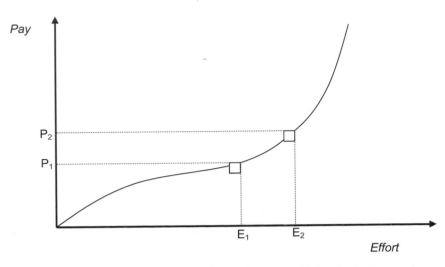

Figure 10 Labour supply curve with mild crowding-out at higher levels of reward

John Stacey Adams – equity theory

A different line of thinking focuses not on needs, expectations or on the difference between intrinsic and extrinsic motivation, but on social comparisons. According to John Stacey Adams we seek a fair balance between what we put into our jobs and what we get out of them.[9] Adams calls these inputs and outputs. We form perceptions of what constitutes a fair balance or trade-off between inputs and outputs by comparing our own situation with other referents (reference points or examples). We are also influenced by our colleagues, friends and partners in establishing these benchmarks and our responses. Inputs include energy, hard work, loyalty, commitment, intelligence, skill, adaptability, tolerance, determination and so on. This is more or less the same as the way we described effort in the previous section. Outputs include financial rewards, recognition, achievement, reputation, praise and thanks, promotion, challenge and interest, responsibility, opportunities for development and personal growth, and so on. Referents may be internal (peers, immediate subordinates, immediate superiors) or external (people doing equivalent jobs in other organisations). There is also a mental referent; does the relationship between my personal inputs and outputs feel fair? Am I being adequately compensated for the effort I am putting in?

If we feel our inputs are fairly rewarded, we will be happy in our work and motivated to keep contributing at the same level.

If we feel that our inputs are fairly and adequately rewarded by outputs, the equity benchmark being subjectively perceived from market norms and other reference points, then we will be happy in our work and motivated to keep contributing at the same (or a higher) level. Note that it is the ratio of inputs

---

9   Adams, J.S. (1965), 'Inequity in Social Exchange', in L. Berkowitz (ed) *Advances in Experimental Social Psychology*, Academic Press, New York.

to outputs in comparison with other people's ratios that is particularly critical, as can be seen from the following formula:

$$Outputs_i / Inputs_i \geq Outputs_r / Inputs_r$$

where:

Outputs$_i$ = individual's outputs

Outputs$_r$ = outputs of other referents

Inputs$_i$ = individual's inputs

Inputs$_r$ = inputs of other referents

If the formula (strictly, an inequality) is true, and the first part of the equation is greater than or equal to the second part of the equation, then the individual will, the theory goes, be happy and motivated. However, if the inequality is false, and the second part of the equation is greater than the first part, then the individual will be unhappy and demotivated. In the second case, the individual may try to balance the equation by reducing inputs, or may make demands for greater reward, or may even seek alternative employment.

Felt-fair principle

Equity theory, along with the felt-fair principle which is derived from it, resonates with many senior executives and well-paid professionals.

Equity theory, as it is known (not to be confused with equity as used in the context of stock plans) along with the felt-fair principle which is derived from it, resonates with many senior executives and well-paid professionals (lawyers, accountants and so on). For example, a large professional partnership for many years shared profits among its partners by applying a matrix which was known only to the firm's top management team. This matrix was heavily skewed towards seniority and tenure as a partner. Details of the matrix and of annual partner income were not widely known within the partnership, though general financial information was available to partners. It was generally known that the range of partner incomes was widely spread. A group of partners began to push for full disclosure of earnings among the partner group. Eventually the firm's management realised that the majority of partners favoured full disclosure and decided to publish details of annual partner income. At the same time it decided to introduce a new partner reward system which was designed much more closely to align performance and relative contribution, rather than tenure. While the new system was widely viewed as a huge improvement on the previous system, there continued to be frequent rumblings about equity between partners. Even though the partners were, by most standards, very well remunerated, individuals continued to say it was how they were paid relative to those who they regarded as their peers that was the critical factor in determining how they felt about their remuneration.

Reciprocity – a variation on equity theory

Reciprocity is a variation on equity theory which examines in particular the relationship between principals and agents. According to reciprocity theory, one of the factors which determines how motivated individuals in agency situations feel is whether they believe that they are receiving a fair share of the profits earned by the principals, given their relative inputs (primarily in the form of human capital and effort in the case of the agents, and financial capital in the case of the principals). In the same way the principals will be angry and dissatisfied if they feel that their agents are exploiting the private knowledge and other privileges which go with their position to extract artificially high rents (an economist's term meaning, broadly, excess profit).

Rodgers and Gago – liberty and equality

In a further development of equity theory, Waymond Rodgers and Susana Gago have identified two key factors in the determination of executive compensation, which they call 'liberty' and 'equality'.[10] Liberty relates to senior executives' need for self-determination; executives wish to feel free to pursue the business goals which they believe to be most important. Equality is closely aligned with equity, though it focuses more on outcomes rather than balancing these with inputs. Liberty and equality are of course political concepts, best understood in a cultural context. While Americans, for example, place a particularly high value on individualism and hence are prepared to accept quite large differences in outcomes for different individuals, this is not the case in some other countries. The compensation policy typical of public corporations in the US tends to place more weight on liberty than equality.

Executives wish to feel free to pursue the business goals which they believe to be most important

CULTURAL DIFFERENCES

It is often said that pay levels and reward structures for senior executives are converging globally, indicative perhaps of an increasingly international market for executive talent. In addition, US companies routinely export pay practices (for example, types of equity plans and levels of award) to executives of foreign subsidiaries, putting pressure on the pay policies of local competitors. And foreign companies acquiring US subsidiaries face huge internal pay inequities, often resolved by increasing home-country executive pay. On average, pay for US CEOs exceeds other countries even after adjusting for special factors, including tax rates, purchasing power parity, public benefits and so on. Interestingly, it would seem that the US premium is less noticeable when it comes to other senior executives.

To understand the cultural issues we need to introduce two new definitions. In an individualistic society the primary focus is on personal self-interest. In

---

10   Rodgers, W. and Gago, S. (2003), 'A Model Capturing Ethics and Executive Compensation', *Journal of Business Ethics*, **48**: 189–202.

a communitarian society the primary focus is on the community. Citizens of an individualistic society would generally say that the only real goal of a company is to make a profit. Citizens of a communitarian society would say that a company, besides making a profit, has a goal of attaining the well-being of various stakeholders, including employees and customers, as well as shareholders.

Circular nature of value resolution

From this distinction we can derive a model called the 'circular nature of value resolution' by Charles Hampden-Turner and Fons Trompenaars (see Figure 11).[11] In individualistic societies, on the one hand, concentration upon self-interest leads to the creation of value for customers and society. In communitarian societies, on the other hand, a focus on customers and society creates value for society as a whole, and therefore by definition benefits particular individuals as well.

US companies routinely export pay practices to executives of foreign subsidiaries, putting pressure on the pay policies of local competitors.

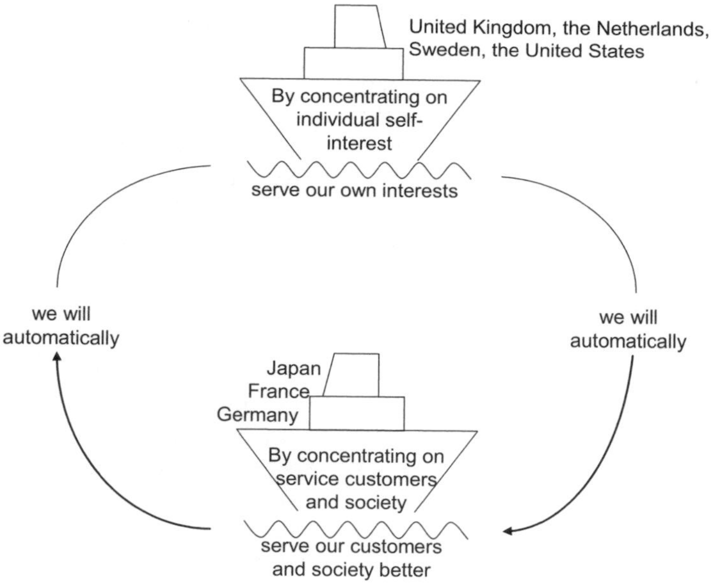

Figure 11 Circular nature of value resolution (after Hampden-Turner and Trompenaars, 1993)

What does this mean for executive pay? In what is primarily an individualistic society, a remuneration strategy designed to incentivise and motivate key executives through high pay should in theory benefit customers and society. In a communitarian society a focus on customer satisfaction and corporate social responsibility should, the theory goes, lead to value creation which also benefits particular individuals. You can begin to see why highly leveraged executive pay strategies are commonly found in an individualistic society

11   Hampden-Turner, C. and Trompenaars, F. (1993), *The Seven Cultures of Capitalism*, Doubleday, New York.

PSYCHOLOGY, SOCIOLOGY AND ORGANISATIONAL BEHAVIOUR

like the US, in contrast with the less generous fixed pay strategies found in a communitarian country like Japan. It is one of the reasons why in the past Japanese senior executives have been so-called 'salary-men', without high-powered equity incentive plans or even big bonuses.

Anglo-Saxon business culture

Let us look in more detail at the kind of business culture which we find in the US and to some extent the UK, compared with the kind of business cultures found in many Continental European countries. The US model is characterised by its culture of individual equity investments, leading to highly dispersed shareholdings, where the profit motive rules supreme and where company directors are forced, by corporate law and commercial practice, to focus above all else on the interests of shareholders. The business culture of many Continental European countries is characterised by significant blockholdings of shares held by banks (for example Germany), wealthy families (for example France and Italy) and the state, where corporate law forces directors to have regard to other stakeholders, most particularly the workforce generally, not just to shareholders. Sandwiched somewhere between the two, in economics as in so many other things, is the UK, with many of the characteristics of the American business culture (highly dispersed shareholdings, a focus on shareholders and so on), but some of the characteristics of Continental Europe. In particular, the UK has an increasing focus on the interests of other stakeholders, most notably employees, illustrated by the adoption of the European Social Chapter in May 1997.

Now let us look in more detail at the typical US corporate model. Shareholdings are widely dispersed. Shareholders have only a tiny fractional interest in company profits. Therefore, they have little incentive (or ability) to discipline management. Executive remuneration is an agency cost. Because pay is not the outcome of a satisfactory arm's-length bargaining process between shareholders and management, executives have scope to influence their remuneration and extract rents, excessive pay and perquisites over and above what would be optimal for shareholders.

The UK has many characteristics of the American business culture, but some of the characteristics of Continental Europe.

One of the ways to address this inherent weakness in contract negotiation is the performance-based pay or incentive contract, including in particular some of the high-powered performance-related equity plans which have emerged over the past few years in an attempt to align more fully the interests of executives (agents) and shareholders (principals). This mechanism, an aspect of agency theory, was described in some detail in Chapter 3. But failing the perfect performance–pay contract, we are left with the need for regulatory intervention to control agency cost. Many of the events in corporate America in the early part of the twenty-first century are indicative of how difficult it is to get this right. The reaction has been a vast expansion of regulatory processes, to the point where concern is now expressed about the extent to which regulation may stifle entrepreneurialism.

Continental Europe

In Continental Europe, executive pay takes on a different complexion, given the large concentration of shareholdings in the hands of banks (Germany), wealthy families (France and Italy) and the state (in the form of either central or local government). This greater concentration of control changes the dynamics of the principal–agent relationship. Blockholding shareholders have significant influence upon management and both the ability and incentive to access information needed to control management's actions.[12] A survey conducted in 2001 showed that in Germany more than 50% of all listed companies were controlled by a single majority block. A similar position existed in Austria, Belgium and Italy for companies other than financial services companies. While family shareholdings form a significant component of Continental European blockholdings, bank influence remains pronounced, particularly in Germany.

Alongside this, the two-tier executive and supervisory board structures found in many Continental European companies means there is the potential for much stronger corporate governance. Another factor is a broader view of which groups are stakeholders in a company. American and English law still ascribes the majority of stakeholder rights to shareholders. In contrast, it has long been a principle of European law that employees have significant stakeholder rights as well. This changes the nature of an executive's obligations and responsibility. The existence, for example, of a works council establishes a different governance axis. The relationship between executive pay and the average pay of employees generally (or at least the rate of increase of the two) comes more closely into focus.

Against this, there is the inevitable problem of board dynamics. Non-executives often feel beholden to the CEO, who may have been instrumental to their appointment. Non-executives of one company may be executives of another, where the remuneration boot, as it were, will be on the other foot. This may be a particular issue in some countries, for example Switzerland, where a relatively small and close group of senior executives has historically acted as executive and non-executive directors of many locally headquartered international companies. Furthermore, there is sometimes a lack of expertise among non-executives about executive pay matters, particularly when it comes to some of the high-powered equity plans which are beginning to find their way into European companies. Finally, there is a shortage of good quality comparative data on executive pay in Continental Europe, a consequence of the degree of secrecy and lack of accounting disclosure historically found in many countries.

In Continental Europe the relationship between executive pay and the average pay of employees (and their pay increases) comes more closely into focus.

---

12   Ferrarini, G., Moloney, N. and Vespro, C. (2003), *Executive Remuneration in the EU: Comparative Law and Practice*, European Corporate Governance Institute Working Paper Series in Law No. 09/2003.

PSYCHOLOGY, SOCIOLOGY AND ORGANISATIONAL BEHAVIOUR

SUMMARY

What motivates executives in an individualistic society like the US is different from what motivates in a communitarian society like Japan.

What insights does organisational behaviour theory give us into how senior executives are motivated, and in particular what is the role of compensation?

- Senior executives have needs too – in terms of Maslow's thinking, the esteem needs of senior executives for status, recognition, achievement and approval, are often highly developed. The role money plays in this is to provide calibration; it allows an objective value to be assigned to subjective qualities of status and achievement.
- The principle of crowding-out – perhaps there comes a point, according to the modified theory of crowding-out, that an individual becomes desensitised to additional rewards, so that a significant increase in pay leads only to a marginal increase in effort.
- The importance of equity – felt-fair applies as much to executives as it does to employees generally. When the CEO of the large UK company mentioned at the start of Chapter 3 talked about market forces he meant that CEOs of similar-sized companies in the US earned more than he did. Related to this is the reciprocity principle. Executives bring their often considerable human capital to bear to generate value for the firm. They may feel that they are entitled to a return on this human capital commensurate to the return that shareholders receive on their financial capital.
- The cultural perspective – what motivates in an individualistic society like the US is different from what motivates in a communitarian society like Japan.

The motivation calculus provides a framework for drawing these various threads together. In designing an effective reward strategy for a group of senior executives you need to examine, individual by individual, their needs, the strength of their feelings about the felt-fair principle and reciprocity, how sensitised (or not) they are to additional monetary rewards, and what alternatively might be necessary to reinforce intrinsic motivation. These things must be combined in the context of a psychological contract which clearly links objectives, achievements and rewards. We will come back to the motivation calculus further in Chapter 7. But before doing so we must turn aside from the rarefied airs of economics and organisational behaviour to more practical things like corporate governance, risk management, compliance, accounting and tax.

CHAPTER 5

Corporate Governance

In 2004 the chief executive of a well-known UK company abruptly resigned after shareholders reacted strongly against a decision by the board to award him a multi-million pound bonus. Shareholders were angered that the bonus was announced following a year when profits fell and at the same time as a new profits warning. So incensed were they that many shareholders voted against the directors' remuneration report, a right they now have under UK company law. The board only narrowly escaped an embarrassing defeat after the company's largest shareholder group decided not to vote down the remuneration report.

If we analyse this case in terms of agency theory, we can see that two things went wrong. The CEO's incentive plan was badly designed, with performance targets that were too easy. He was entitled to collect a significant proportion of the maximum bonus despite falling profits and shareholder returns. On top of this, corporate governance processes went awry. In the eyes of shareholders the remuneration committee failed to exercise proper control over executive pay. It was no great surprise that the chairman of the remuneration committee also resigned.

'Corporate governance' refers to the organisational structures, policies and procedures which govern the relationship between a company and its investors.

WHAT IS CORPORATE GOVERNANCE?

'Corporate governance' refers to the organisational structures, policies and procedures which govern the relationship between a company (particularly its senior executives) and its investors (particularly shareholders). These structures, policies and procedures relate principally to three things:

- Information – what is available to shareholders, what is available to senior management, how is information which is available only to senior management to be properly used?
- Decision making – how are key decisions made, which decisions must be referred to shareholders, and so on?
- Conflicts of interest – how can the parties ensure that proper decisions are made when the interests of executives and shareholders are potentially in

conflict, for example when it comes to the question of how profits are to be shared?

Part of the controversy over CEO compensation comes from a perception that CEOs effectively set their own pay levels. In practice, the reward arrangements for the CEO and other senior executives are the preserve of the remuneration or compensation committee, a sub-committee of the main board comprising entirely of independent non-executive directors. Compensation committees are keenly aware of the conflicts of interest arising between managers and shareholders over executive pay, and of the level of scrutiny exercised by outside shareholders, investor protection groups and the public generally. Nevertheless, there is no doubt that in many companies CEOs and other top managers exert a degree of influence on both the level and structure of their pay.

Initial recommendations for pay levels and new incentive plans typically come from a company's human resources department, often working in conjunction with outside consultants. These recommendations are usually sent to top management for approval and revision before being delivered to the remuneration committee for consideration. In the US the CEO typically participates in the compensation committee's deliberations, except for discussions relating to the CEO's own pay. In the UK and Europe, where separation of responsibilities between a non-executive chairman and an executive CEO is now the norm, there is an added safeguard in that it is the chairman's job to steer senior executive reward proposals through the remuneration committee and the board. The committee either accepts the recommendations or sends them back for revision. If accepted, the committee passes the recommendations to the main board for approval. All major decisions related to top-level pay are now passed as a matter of course through the remuneration committee. Increasingly, the committee may conduct its own market studies of competitive pay levels and retain its own compensation experts.

United Kingdom

Many commentators consider the UK to have led the way on corporate governance when it comes to directors' remuneration. A series of public reports over the last decade, commencing with the Cadbury report in 1992 and taken forward by Greenbury (1995), Hampel (1998), Turnbull (1999), Higgs (2003) and Smith (also 2003) has given rise to a comprehensive system of corporate governance, a key part of which relates to directors' remuneration. This has three main elements.

- Statutory requirements, more particularly the Directors' Remuneration Report Regulations 2002, require all quoted companies to publish a directors' remuneration report with their annual accounts; this must contain a statement of the company's policy on directors' remuneration as well as individual disclosure of salaries, bonuses, pension benefits, share plans and other long-term incentives.

- Stock exchange regulations, including the Combined Code on Corporate Governance which used to be annexed to the UK Listing Rules and is now published by the Financial Reporting Council, apply to all companies quoted on the London Stock Exchange (typically on a 'comply or explain basis'); among other things the code requires listed companies to establish remuneration committees composed of independent directors, and the roles of chairman and CEO to be separated.
- Institutional investor guidelines, issued by the Association of British Insurers and National Association of Pension Funds, deal in particular with bonuses, share incentives, performance conditions, remuneration policy, benchmarking, service contracts and terminations.

Within the UK model we find three themes which will occur again in our examination of the corporate governance regimes of other jurisdictions:

- Full disclosure – an obligation on companies to provide very detailed information about directors' pay, information being a key ingredient in the economists' cookbook for the efficient operation of markets;
- Separation of responsibilities – between the chairman (who runs the board) and CEO (who runs the business of the company) as well as between independent directors (who represent the interests of all the shareholders) and executive directors (the company's management);
- Due process – particularly in the setting of remuneration policy and individual executive director's compensation packages by an independent remuneration committee.

European Union

The executive pay question has not historically been so contentious in other parts of Europe, where (with certain notable exceptions) executives are not generally paid at UK levels and certainly not at US levels. Perhaps this is a consequence of the greater concentration of control among Continental European companies. But things are changing. In May 2003 the European Commission adopted an action plan announcing measures to modernise company law and enhance corporate governance in the European Union. The action plan recognised the need for shareholders to be able to appreciate fully the relationship between the performance of the company and the level of remuneration of directors, as well as to make decisions on the remuneration items linked to the share price. In the autumn of 2004 the European Commission recommended that, each year, firms release a remuneration statement containing a statement of remuneration policy and a breakdown of all the components of their directors' fixed and variable pay. The recommendation includes provisions requiring the remuneration statement to be put to a shareholder vote at the annual general meeting, for the remuneration policy to be a separate item on the meeting agenda, and for all equity-based incentive arrangements to be subject to prior shareholder approval. It urged European countries to take suitable measures by the end of June 2006.

Executive pay has not historically been so contentious in Continental Europe, where executives are not generally paid at UK or US levels.

France

French best practices on corporate governance are described in three reports – the first and second Viénot reports, produced by two committees chaired by M. Marc Viénot in 1995 and 1999, and the Bouton report, produced by a committee chaired by M. Daniel Bouton in 2002. These best practice guidelines have been endorsed and promoted by the main French employers' associations Association Francaise des Entreprises Privées (AFEP) and Mouvement des Entreprises de France (MEDEF).

French law requires all listed companies each year to publish a remuneration report with their annual report and accounts. This must contain details by individual of the total compensation and benefits awarded to the company's corporate officers (*mandataires sociaux*). Where there is a unitary board (*conseil d'administration*) the total directors' remuneration is fixed by the shareholders' general meeting; the board of directors then determines the allocation of this amount among its members. The Bouton report recommends the creation of a remuneration committee for this purpose. In 2005 the Breton Law introduced additional formalities and reporting requirements, including a provision requiring certain key executives to disclose all share transactions to the Financial Markets Authority (Autorité des Marchés Financiers), as well as new rules relating to termination payments and supplemental pension schemes.

French law requires all listed companies each year to publish a remuneration report with their annual report and accounts.

Germany

On the face of it German corporate governance structures would appear to be quite robust. In particular, it is a legal requirement that a separate supervisory board comprising both shareholder and employee representatives oversees the activities of a company's management board. However, some commentators have questioned the effectiveness of German supervisory boards, especially because the shareholders' representatives are often former executives of the company. In the case of more than half of Germany's top 30 listed companies, the chairman of the supervisory board is a former CEO. Their independence and objectivity may, it is argued, be compromised as a result.[1] On the question of disclosure, in 2003 the Cromme Commission (which gave rise to the German Corporate Governance Code) recommended that companies publish details of the remuneration of individual board members. In the past they have only been required to release aggregate figures. Prior to 2005 less than half of the 30 companies on the German stock market's DAX index had complied with these requirements. In July 2005 the German Federal Council passed a new law obliging German stock corporations to disclose individually what management board members earn. However, the law contains an opt-out allowing companies not to disclose individual management board remuneration if non-disclosure is approved by a 75% majority of shareholders at a general meeting.

---

1   See for example 'Corporate Governance in Germany: A Model Out of Time?', *The Economist*, 29 January, 2005.

Switzerland

Switzerland is currently home to eleven of the world's largest companies, and executive remuneration at the most senior end is second only to the US. Even Switzerland, with its historical concerns for individual privacy, has seen an increased focus on disclosure and other aspects of corporate governance. A panel of experts was set up by the Swiss employer's association in cooperation with the SWX Swiss Stock Exchange in 2000. The panel published the Swiss Code of Best Practice in Corporate Governance in March 2002. This in turn led to the Exchange's Corporate Governance Directive which entered into force on 1 July 2002. While the directive does not require individual disclosure of directors' and senior executives' compensation, the Swiss code does adopt many other best practice guidelines which apply elsewhere in Europe.

In 2005 the Swiss parliament approved new rules which, if enacted, will extend these disclosure requirements significantly after 2007. In particular the total compensation of individual members of the board of directors and the advisory board, if there is one, would have to be disclosed on a named basis.

United States

In the US, the literature is full of stories of excessive pay in companies where corporate governance failed. For example, it is reported that in the year 2000 total compensation for the 200 highest-compensated executives at Enron was $1.4 billion, an average of $7 million per executive. Corporate governance in the US has relied more on disclosure than processes and structures. The required level of disclosure of the pay, benefits and incentives of the top-five named executives is very extensive – there are few places to hide – and these requirements may be extended in the future if proposals put forward by the Securities and Exchange Commission in January 2006 are adopted. But having a compensation committee composed entirely of independent directors has only become a requirement in the last few years, and while recent New York Stock Exchange and NASDAQ rulings are increasing the independence of boards, it is still common practice in the US for the role of chairman and CEO to be combined. This concentration of power in one place, in contrast with the European model where the CEO runs the company and oversees operational management and the chairman runs the board and oversees the CEO, is regarded by some commentators as a critical deficiency in the American corporate governance model.

The required level of disclosure of the pay, benefits and incentives of the US top five named executives is very extensive.

Of course the American brand of capitalism has always been tolerant of high rewards for individual success and massive differentials between a company's senior executives and other employees, in contrast with more collectivist cultures found for example in Continental Europe and Japan. Perhaps some clues about this can again be found in the ultimatum game (see the beginning of Chapter 4). Experimental game theorists have found that American proposers in the ultimatum game on average make lower offers, and that American responders are more likely to accept these than is the case in, say, Canada or Japan.

Table 2 Comparison of the main corporate governance rules for executive pay

	France	Germany	Switzerland	UK	US
Is individual disclosure of directors' remuneration required?	Yes	Recommended by the German Corporate Governance Code. Now also a legal requirement, though subject to an opt-out provision	Highest-paid director and aggregate of all directors' remuneration only. Individual disclosures may be required from 2007 if provisional new laws are enacted	Yes	Yes, currently for the top five executives
Are shareholders entitled to vote on directors' remuneration?	Yes, in respect of the aggregate amount only	Yes, for the supervisory board and in respect of the aggregate amount only	No	Yes, but the effect of the vote is advisory only	No
Is shareholders' approval required for stock-based incentive plans?	Yes	No, approval is required for the issuing of shares generally, not specific plans	No, approval is required for the issuing of shares generally, not specific plans	Yes	Yes
Must a remuneration committee comprised of independent directors approve executive remuneration proposals?	Recommended	Supervisory board can delegate responsibilities to a compensation committee	Recommended	Recommended – 'comply or explain'	Recommended
Is it normal to have a single or two-tier board?	Single-tier, occasionally two-tier	Two-tier, required by law	Two-tier boards required by Swiss banking law for all banks. Many other Swiss companies have a board of directors and separate executive board	Single-tier	Single-tier
Is separation of roles between the chairman and CEO required?	No	Yes	Required for banks. Otherwise not required, but increasingly common in practice	Recommended –'comply or explain'	No, though 'lead non-executive directors' are increasingly common
What is the recommended maximum length of directors' contracts?	4 years recommended; 6-year limit required by law	Appointments to supervisory board are for a maximum of 5 years	4 years recommended	1 year recommended	None, although severance or change-in-control arrangements often imply a 3-year notice period

TRENDS IN CORPORATE GOVERNANCE

This review of corporate governance practices across a number of key jurisdictions has shown some important trends:

- towards ever greater disclosure of executive compensation;
- the increasing importance of remuneration committees;
- a stronger role for independent directors either in a one-tier or two-tier board and management committee structures;
- limits on executives' contractual terms of office;
- separating the two most senior board roles to ensure too much power does not rest in one place.

The trend is towards ever greater disclosure of executive compensation and the increasing importance of remuneration committees.

Further information on the corporate governance regimes in the UK, France, Germany, Switzerland and the US, homes to around 300 of the world's 500 largest companies,[2] is found in the Appendices. A comparative summary is provided in Table 2 on the opposite page.

RISK MANAGEMENT AND COMPLIANCE

Increasingly linked with governance are two other corporate processes: risk management and compliance. In the context of executive pay, risk management has three main dimensions.

The first is the risk of failure of strategy execution because the company's business strategy and remuneration plans are not properly aligned. Consider the story of a London market insurance company, which employed two senior underwriters for its marine and aviation businesses. In the 1970s they underwrote a mixed book of business, including a category of risk which subsequently became known as product-related hazards. These policies had what is called in the insurance world a 'long tail'; claims on the policies only came to light many years, sometimes ten or more, after the policies had been written. In the 1980s, after a takeover by a large overseas financial institution, the company changed its underwriting policy, but the two principal underwriters remained in post. At about this time the company entered into new incentive contracts with its lead underwriting staff, including the marine and aviation underwriters. These contracts rewarded the underwriters with cash bonuses linked to the success of their current underwriting activities. The new underwriting approach was very successful, the company's new book of business performed well, and the underwriters earned substantial reward from the incentive programme. Unfortunately, at the same time claims on the old book of business stacked up at an alarming rate. The company was exposed through its reinsurance programmes to product liability claims relating to asbestosis, as well as a number of other industrial diseases. So significant were the claims that the company's parent eventually decided to cap its exposure

---

2   'Global 500 Companies', *Fortune Magazine*, 25 July, 2005.

by putting its subsidiary into liquidation. The principal underwriters, now more or less of retirement age, had earned multi-million pound bonuses over a number of years while the company they worked for suffered catastrophic losses on business they had written years before.

The second is in the area of reputational risk. In the last few years there have been a number of occasions when companies' reputations have suffered because of unfavourable public responses to executive pay proposals. Reactions like this can depress a company's share price. There have also been instances when shareholder pressure over pay has forced senior executives to resign at short notice without time for proper succession planning.

There have been instances when shareholder pressure over pay has forced senior executives to resign at short notice without proper succession planning.

The third area of risk is of legal, regulatory or tax non-compliance. In the US, quoted companies are required by the Securities and Exchange Commission (SEC) to file proxy statements giving detailed information about the pay and terms of employment of the company's top five executives. Failure to comply within the time limits or, worse still, disclosing incorrect information can result in stiff penalties. In the UK, listed companies are required to provide full details of their directors' compensation in a remuneration report, which is published along with the company's annual financial statements. The Listing Rules of the London Stock Exchange require all long-term incentive plans involving awards to directors or the issue of new shares to be approved by shareholders before any awards are made. Failure to do this may result in the company being censured, various sanctions and, in extreme cases, the company's listing being suspended. There are many more examples, in the UK, the US, Continental Europe and other parts of the world.

The lesson is clear: regulatory authorities are determined that executives' actions regarding their own pay and benefits are made fully transparent to shareholders, and stiff penalties will be applied if the rules are not followed. Company executives' personal tax filings are also increasingly a matter of great sensitivity. No company with an eye to its corporate and social responsibility ratings would wish to find its executives being publicly criticised for aggressive personal tax planning, or worse, for tax fraud, yet a number of companies in the US have recently found themselves in this position.

Tax and Accounting

Twenty-five years ago the biggest component of executive compensation was cash in the form of salary and bonuses. Since then stock option grants have come to dominate the pay of top executives in North America and most of Europe. By 1999, for example, stock options accounted for more than half of total CEO compensation in the largest US companies and about 30% of senior executives' pay.[1] This massive increase in the incidence of share option plans gives a number of important insights into the significance of tax and accounting in executive reward.

Some of the reasons for the exponential growth in the use of share options are entirely consistent with agency theory. By increasing the number of shares in which executives have an interest and thereby linking executive reward to growth in shareholder value, option grants have strengthened the link between pay and performance. But share options are complex financial instruments. Their economic characteristics, particular in volatile markets, are often poorly understood by the companies who grant them and the executives who hold them. Why have options been so much more popular than share awards, restricted stock or deferred cash bonuses, all of which can equally well be used to align the interests of shareholders and executives? And why, for example, in the US have fixed-price options been the norm when so many commentators have advocated the merits of indexed-price or performance-related options? In the UK performance options are now the norm; executives can only exercise their options if certain corporate financial performance targets have been met.

Option grants have strengthened the link between pay and performance.

APB 25

In 1993 a ferocious row broke out in the US financial community about a proposed new financial accounting standard. In one corner was the Financial Accounting Standards Board (FASB) who wanted to adopt a new standard for accounting for stock options. In the other corner were many corporations and

---

1   Rappaport, A. (1999), 'New Thinking in How to Link Executive Pay to Performance', *Harvard Business Review*, March–April 1999, 91–101.

investors, who wanted to keep the status quo. At the time, generally accepted accounting practice was to account for stock options in accordance with rules set out in Accounting Practices Board opinion number 25 (APB 25). APB 25 relied on an accounting fiction. It assumed that the cost of a fixed option (an option over a fixed number of shares with a predetermined exercise or 'strike' price) was negligible if the strike price was equal to the share price at the grant date. Accordingly, no expense had to be recognised over the vesting period of the option. Instead, in effect the economic cost of options was to be borne indirectly by shareholders through the dilution in the value of their shares which occurred when options were exercised. For example, if an option over 10000 shares with a strike price of $5 per share was exercised when the share price was $10, all shareholders theoretically suffered a proportionate reduction in the value of their shares equal to the economic cost (($10 - $5) × 10000 = $50000).

Variable options

There were two important exceptions. First, if an option was granted with a strike price which was below market value, then the discount had to be expensed over the vesting period of the option. Second, an accounting charge did arise in the case of variable options, where either the share price or the number of shares arising on exercise was not fixed at the grant date. In this case an expense had to be recognised each time the exercise price or number of shares arising on exercise was determined. For example, let us imagine that an option over 10000 shares was granted with a strike price of $5. The option was subject to a performance condition: if growth in earnings per share (EPS) exceeded 7.5% per annum on average, then the option could be exercised after three years over up to 50% of the underlying shares; if growth in EPS exceeded 10% per annum then the option could be exercised in full. In the event, after three years average EPS growth was more than 7.5% but less than 10%, so only 5000 shares were released. An accounting charge arose equal to the share price at the third anniversary of grant, say $9, less the strike price of $5, multiplied by the number of shares issue, in other words ($9 - $5) × 5000 = $20000.

Because of the marked difference in accounting treatment between fixed and variable options, fixed options have invariably been preferred in the US. To illustrate the effect on the design of incentive plans let's consider the example of a reinsurance company based in London which was acquired from its majority shareholder by a private equity house in the mid-1990s. The private equity house's plan was to allow the existing management team to run the company for a few years before seeking an initial public offering (IPO) on the New York Stock Exchange, where reinsurance company shares have generally been priced more highly than in London. Accordingly, they needed to incentivise management during the pre-IPO period, and were attracted by the merits of performance options – options whose exercisability was dependent on the company meeting various financial performance targets. The investors knew that if they managed the listing process correctly then the share price should rise at the time of the IPO; they wanted to reward senior executives only to the extent that this was warranted by management's stewardship of the company in the pre-IPO period. Unfortunately, however, performance options are deemed to be variable options under APB 25, so that a significant accounting charge would have arisen in the company's accounts during the pre-IPO period, highly undesirable as far as the private equity house was concerned as the price at which their shares would be sold in the IPO would in part depend on reported earnings in the years leading up to listing. As a result, the private equity house decided to drop the performance conditions and to award management simple fixed-price options. Even though the company's senior executives might benefit simply because the investors obtained a good price on the IPO, rather than as a result of their own good stewardship, because no accounting charge would arise in the case of fixed-price options the private equity house quite understandably preferred to take this approach.

By the early 1990s the FASB had come to recognise the theoretical flaws in the APB 25 approach. It defied financial logic that less costly variable options had to be expensed while more costly fixed options did not. Furthermore the FASB believed that the working assumption on which APB 25 was based (that an option had no value if it was granted with an exercise price at least equal to the current market value) was no longer sustainable. Accordingly, in June 1993 it issued an exposure draft recommending that all stock options should be valued at the time of issue using an accepted option valuation methodology, such as the 'Black-Scholes pricing model'. The Black-Scholes model, named after Fischer Black and Myron Scholes, two Nobel prize-winning economists, takes account of many factors that affect the value of an option – the stock price, the exercise price, the maturity date, prevailing interest rates, the company's dividend rate and, most importantly, the volatility of the company's stock. The last factor, stock price volatility, is particularly important as it varies significantly from company to company: the higher the expected volatility of a company's stock price, the higher the value of an option. This is because the holder of an option will receive the full value of any upside change, while the downside risk is limited: an option's pay-off hits zero once the stock price equals the exercise price, but remains zero if the stock price falls further. The downside risk is capped while the upside opportunity is in theory unlimited.

FAS 123

The FASB proposed that the value of an option should be calculated at the date of grant, and this value should be expensed over the expected life of the option. Thus an option granted over 10000 shares at an exercise price of, say $10, with a Black-Scholes value of, say, $3 and which vested fully after, say, three years, would result in an annual accounting cost of $10000 for the three years following the option's grant. The implications of this new practice would have been enormous. For example one Fortune top-100 company which did eventually decide to restate its accounts on a FAS 123 basis increased its annual compensation expense by around $7.5 billion over a period of three years leading up to the change, reducing total profits for the years in question by around 35%. As a result companies and investors lobbied

It defied logic that less costly variable options had to be expensed while more costly fixed options did not.

both the FASB and the US Senate, arguing that implementing the exposure draft would significantly damage the competitiveness of American companies compared with companies in Europe, which would still account for options on the old basis. In the end there was a rather peculiar compromise, set out in an accounting standard known as FAS 123. FAS 123 recommended that companies should expense the cost of an option over the option's vesting period, but alternatively allowed companies to prepare their accounts on the old APB 25 basis, provided that in a note to the accounts they disclosed the effect on earnings had the option been valued at the date of grant and expensed in the manner which had been proposed in the exposure draft. Unsurprisingly most companies chose to adopt the alternative accounting treatment permitted by FAS 123.

A particular method of accounting for one element of compensation can significantly affect a company's reward strategy.

In other parts of the world share option accounting has generally followed the same underlying approach as APB 25: options granted with an exercise price which was at least equal to the share price at the date of grant were assumed to have a negligible cost. Accordingly, no accounting charge arose. However, accounting bodies in other countries have not applied the APB's distinction between fixed and variable options, so that performance plans and other variable options did not give rise to an accounting expense. This has meant that, for example, in the UK performance-related share options have become the norm, particularly given the encouragement they have received from institutional investor bodies, the Association of British Insurers and the National Association of Pensions funds, whose members jointly hold around 30% of shares listed on the London Stock Exchange.

The reason for recounting the story of the FAS 123 controversy at some length is because it shows how a particular method of accounting for one element of compensation can significantly affect a company's reward strategy. Would stock options ever have been so prevalent if it had not been for the favourable way in which they were reported? It is probably no coincidence that the Fortune top-100 company mentioned previously, which voluntarily decided to adopt FAS 123, did this at the same time as it decided to abandon stock options and replace them with performance-related restricted shares and other kinds of restricted stock. But it is not just the accounting treatment which has supported the widespread use of share options; the tax code applicable to stock options in many countries has encouraged the use of stock options to reward executives by providing various positive tax incentives.

TAX RULES ENCOURAGING THE USE OF STOCK OPTIONS

Stock options are a relatively unusual form of deferred compensation in the sense that the holder has considerable discretion in choosing when to realise taxable income. In most jurisdictions around the world the granting of an option does not constitute a taxable event. Generally tax only arises when options are exercised, at which point income tax is payable by the option-holder on the difference (known as the spread) between the strike price and the value of the shares at the exercise date. In the US, incentive stock options (ISOs) benefit from a further tax advantage in that no tax is payable until the underlying shares are sold, at which point the total gain (the sale price less the exercise price) is taxed as a capital gain. Similar treatment is afforded to approved share options in the UK and France.

ISOs suffer one disadvantage in comparison with non-qualified stock options (NQSOs). In the case of NQSOs the employer generally receives a corporate tax deduction for the spread. This is not available for ISOs, and in many cases has been sufficient to make NQSOs more tax efficient in overall terms than ISOs. Probably for this reason the use of ISOs in the US has been quite limited in practice.

Restricted stock – tax and accounting

Contrast this with the way in which restricted stock awards have generally been taxed and accounted for. Restricted shares have a value for accounting purposes when they are issued. This value is treated as a compensation expense which must be charged against earnings. Most employers spread the compensation expense over the period ending when the stock has fully vested. Normally there is no tax on the recipient at the time of the award of restricted stock. Instead the executive is taxed at the time of vesting; in US terminology, when there is no longer a substantial risk of forfeiture. The taxable amount is the value of the shares once all the restrictions have lifted. The effect is not dissimilar to the way that stock options are taxed, with the important difference that the restricted stock holder does not have the flexibility of choosing when to crystallise a tax charge.

New accounting rules – IFRS 2

It can be seen how the popularity of share options is in large part the result of their favourable tax and accounting treatment in many parts of the world. Unlike restricted shares, stock options have in practice been regarded as essentially free from an accounting perspective, and have offered an attractive way of deferring taxable income. However, things are changing as regulators and accounting standard setters push for ever more transparent disclosure. In many countries the old way of accounting for stock options has, from 1 January 2005, become a thing of the past. International financial reporting standard number 2 (IFRS 2) requires the fair value of a share-based payment transaction to be measured at the date on which an equity instrument is awarded, and expensed over the instrument's vesting period. This rule applies equally to shares, restricted shares and share options. In the case of share options fair value must be estimated using a suitable option pricing model. The Black-Scholes formula is explicitly referred to in the standard's rubric as a pricing model which it may be appropriate to use in some cases, although IFRS 2 is relatively cautious regarding its suitability in all circumstances.

IFRS2 requires the fair value of a share-based payment to be measured at the award date and expensed over the instrument's vesting period.

The impact of IFRS 2 is more or less the same as the approach which was recommended, but not mandated, by FAS 123 in 1993, and effectively puts restricted stock and share options on the same footing from an accounting perspective. Although international financial reporting standards have now been adopted as the norm in most European countries and many other parts of the world, they do not apply in North America, where US generally accepted accounting rules as promulgated by the FASB still apply. Nevertheless, in part to ensure convergence with international accounting standards and in part recognising that over 750 US public companies had voluntarily chosen to adopt the FAS 123 fair-value approach, in December 2004 the FASB issued a revised version of FAS 123, known as FAS 123R. Among other things, this makes the expensing of stock options mandatory after June 2005, so that the alternative approach of disclosing the effect on earnings of expensing stock options only in a note to the financial statements will no longer be available.

TAX RULES DESIGNED TO RESTRAIN EXECUTIVE COMPENSATION

An example of a negative tax incentive is found in section 162(m) of the US Internal Revenue Code. This provides that compensation paid to the CEO and the next four highest-paid executives in a firm in excess of $1 million is not tax deductible unless certain conditions are satisfied. These conditions are that the payments in excess of $1 million must be made under a performance-based plan and that the plan must have been approved in advance by shareholders. When this measure was introduced in the US by Congress in 1993 its proponents argued that it would reduce what they regarded as excessive executive compensation by raising the cost to the corporation. It would also, they believed, encourage companies to establish performance-related incentive plans for senior executives. Evidence gathered since the introduction of section 162(m) suggests that the limits on the deductibility of fixed pay over and above the $1 million cap has led companies paying executives at levels close to the cap to restrict salary increases and in some cases to enhance the performance-related components of their compensation arrangements. The effect on the overall level of executive pay, looked at in terms of companies generally, is less noticeable, casting doubt on the effectiveness of the legislation in constraining executive pay.[2]

Compensation paid to US CEOs and their next four highest-paid executives in excess of $1 million are typically not tax deductible.

An illustration of this can be found by examining the accounts of another Fortune top-100 company. In 1996 the company's shareholders voted on a plan for the pay of its chairman and CEO covering the five years to 2001. However, the approval then lapsed and was not renewed until 2004. In the two intervening years the chairman received bonuses of $5 million (2002) and $6.5 million (2003), in addition to an annual salary of $1 million. The

---

2   Rose, N.L and Wolfram, C. (2000), 'Has the "Million-Dollar Cap" Affected CEO Pay?', *American Economic Review*, May 2000, 197–202.

company's effective corporate tax rate was around 30% in both years. This means that that company could have saved tax of nearly $3.5 million if the bonus payments had been made under an incentive plan which had been pre-approved by shareholders; an odd result, and not on the face of it an example of best practice when it comes to corporate governance.

Golden parachutes

Another US example of an attempt to restrain a particular kind of compensation payment is found in section 280G of the Internal Revenue Code. This section deals with termination payment made to executives when a company is taken over (known as 'golden parachutes'). Congress viewed excessive golden parachute payments as detrimental to the interests of shareholders and an unreasonable deterrent to corporate acquisitions. Accordingly, legislation was enacted in an attempt to restrict the widespread use of such arrangements.

If a golden parachute payment exceeds three times the average annual taxable compensation of an executive calculated over a period of five years preceding the year in which the employing company is taken over, then the excess over and above once times the average annual compensation is subject to a 20% excise tax. This is on top of the usual income taxes that would be assessed. In addition, the corporation cannot claim a deduction for any excess payments when computing its own corporate income tax liability.

American Jobs Creation Act of 2004

A more recent attempt to use the tax code to place restraints on executive compensation can be found in the American Jobs Creation Act of 2004. Suddenly aware, apparently, of the aggressive deferred compensation arrangements that some corporations and their managers were using to postpone personal income tax, the US Congress finally decided to act. The new legislation imposes tax on an accruals basis on senior executives whose deferred compensation arrangements fail any one of a number of tests. In addition, a flat rate 20% surtax is levied on any non-compliant plan.

The three key tests specified in the legislation are as follows:

- An election to defer compensation must be made in the tax year preceding the year in which compensation is earned;
- Deferred compensation cannot be secured by holding assets offshore or by restricting creditor access to assets underpinning the plan in the event of the company's insolvency;
- Compensation can only be paid in accordance with a predetermined schedule of payments, or earlier on separation from service, death, disability, change of control over the sponsoring company, or some other unforeseen emergency; the compensation plan cannot allow the acceleration of payments in any other circumstances.

The American Jobs Creation Act of 2004 imposes tax on an accruals basis on senior executives whose deferred compensation arrangements fail any one of a number of tests.

TAX AND
ACCOUNTING

Deferred compensation which satisfies these rules is taxed in the same way as previously, before the new law came into effect: an executive is liable to personal income tax only when payment is received and the company can generally deduct the payment for corporate income tax purposes in the year in which the payment is made. In effect, the corporation pays tax on investment income attributable to the deferred compensation as it rolls up. Executives receive a net-of-tax investment return unless the company, at the expense of shareholders, decides to offer a gross return.

Whether the new rules will have an impact on the way corporations use deferred compensation has yet to be seen. At least one leading research body, the Urban-Brookings Tax Policy Center in Washington DC, believes it will not, because Congress has failed to pursue a policy of strict neutrality on the way tax is levied on current and deferred compensation, which could only really be achieved if deferred compensation was taxed on an accruals basis.[3]

Accountants have struggled to reach a consensus on how retirement benefit plans should be reported in a company's annual accounts.

PENSIONS

Accounting for pensions and other retirement benefits is one of the most difficult topics in financial reporting. For many years accountants across the world have struggled to reach a consensus on how retirement benefit plans should be reported in a company's annual accounts. In the US, prospective retirement benefits payable to each of the top-five named executive officers must be disclosed in annual proxy statements. These are public documents which must be lodged each year with the SEC. The disclosures must be made in such a way that all benefits to which each of the named officers will be entitled to receive after retirement can be readily determined. In the UK, listed companies are required to give details of the pension entitlements of individual executive directors. Disclosures must include the amount of the accrued annual pension at the start and end of the year, transfer values (the amount which would have to be paid over to another pension plan if a departing executive chose to transfer his pension to his new employer), any lump sums paid to executives who have recently retired and so on. In the case of defined contribution schemes, it is the contributions paid or payable in respect of each executive director which have to be reported.

The tax treatment of pensions is if anything even more complex than the accounting and this is not the place for a detailed review. In many countries pensions are taxed on a 'gross-gross-net' basis: pension contributions are made by employers and employees out of pre-tax income; investment returns which accrue to the pension fund are broadly tax-free; however, pensions and other retirement benefits are generally taxed as ordinary income. Various jurisdictions, including the US and the UK, have placed restrictions on the amounts that can be set aside and accrue income on a tax-free basis, no doubt

---

3   Doran, M. (2004), *Executive Compensation Reform and the Limits of Tax Policy*, Urban-Brookings Tax Policy Center, Discussion Paper No. 18, November 2004.

with an eye to curbing top-up executive pensions. To date, however, evidence suggests that the cost of these constraints falls on shareholders; companies are often prepared to bear the additional tax costs of top-up pensions themselves, rather than allowing the costs to be borne by senior executives. Various justifications are given for this. Companies may argue that it is necessary to preserve equity between executives; some long-standing executives have generous pension arrangements which are protected under an old tax regime. It may be a senior-level recruitment issue: offering a generous top-up pension may be necessary to induce a top manager to leave behind an established tax-protected pension arrangement which they have with their previous employer. However, some economists argue that this is another example of an agency cost – of unequal bargaining positions as between company managers and shareholders.

SUMMARY

It is hard to avoid the conclusion that accounting and tax factors influence executive pay when the effect is positive for executives or the company, but not when the effect is negative. Negative tax incentives, offered for example by the US government, have generally had an insignificant impact in terms of restraining executive compensation. It is also hard not to conclude that unintended consequences prevail over intended ones: the historical accounting treatment of stock options has been a much greater inducement to companies to provide long-term incentives in the form of options than any of the positive tax incentives.

The moral for governments, accounting standard setters and regulators is the same. They should pursue policies which are broadly neutral as between different ways of remunerating executives. They should ensure that all compensation costs are expensed in computing earnings. They should insist on full disclosure of all the main components of executive reward. Companies should be encouraged to decide on remuneration strategies for top managers according to what will have the most positive incentive effect, not the tax and accounting treatment.

The moral for companies and executives is more paradoxical. While accounting and tax anomalies remain, it would be silly to suggest that reward strategies should not seek to exploit any available arbitrage opportunities. Yet companies should ensure that this is not at the expense of the design features necessary to achieve the required incentive effect. They should also make the working assumption that governments, standard setters and regulators will pursue policies which do not favour or discriminate against particular ways of rewarding top managers, and that a more neutral tax and accounting environment will eventually be achieved in all major jurisdictions.

Accounting and tax factors influence executive pay when the effect is positive for executives or the company, but not when the effect is negative.

TAX AND
ACCOUNTING

Turning Theory Into Practice

'**I**need action, not theories,' said the remuneration committee chairman. In a similar vein, Keith Grint, in the introduction to his book *Fuzzy Management*,[1] recites the following verse:

> *Theory is where you know everything and nothing works;*
> *Practice is where everything works but nobody knows why;*
> *Here we combine theory with practice;*
> *Nothing works and nobody knows why.*

Of course Keith Grint, a leading business management theorist in his own right, is being ironic: it is as wrong to say that by combining theory and practice 'nothing works and nobody knows why' as it would be to say that 'everything works and everybody knows why'. Kurt Lewin, the eminent psychologist, put it rather better when he said, 'There is nothing so practical as a good theory.' Good theories, sensibly interpreted, do help to shed light on actual practice. In this spirit, the purpose of the final chapter is to take the various theoretical insights from the earlier parts of this book and to turn them into principles which can be applied in practice.

'There is nothing so pratical as a good theory' – Kurt Lewin

In the introduction we set out a way of examining executive pay under four main headings: economic models; psychology, sociology and organisational behaviour; corporate governance; and tax and accounting. Each of these areas has given us a number of significant insights into how to design or appraise a total reward strategy for senior executives. These main insights fall under the headings of, respectively, the incentive contract, motivation calculus, the key role of corporate governance (including risk management and compliance) and the importance of fully understanding the tax and accounting implications of executive reward plans (see Figure 12).

---

1   Grint, K. (1997), *Fuzzy Management: Contemporary Ideas and Practices at Work*, Oxford University Press, Oxford.

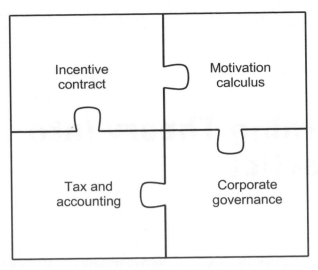

Figure 12   Framework for designing senior executive reward strategies

INCENTIVE CONTRACTS

A critical insight from Chapter 3 is the importance of the incentive contract in aligning the different interests of shareholders and top managers. Incentive contracts need to be thought of as part of a broad picture of value creation. We explained at the end of Chapter 1 how creating firm value should be the primary objective of a company. This is a fundamental assumption, but is not a mission statement or a strategy. This governing objective should be complemented by both a statement of the company's corporate vision and a business strategy in order to bring the underlying objective to life and to motivate the people in the organisation to create value. To support the corporate vision statement and business strategy, companies should develop a reward strategy for their most senior executives. This must reflect and be aligned with the governing objective, vision statement and strategy.

Reward plans must be understandable to the people they cover and comprehensible to others, including shareholders, in order to help build trust.

The incentive contract has many dimensions. It will inevitably be complex but must nevertheless be capable of being explained and understood. Simplicity in remuneration planning is an important principle: reward plans must be understandable to the people they cover if they are to be effective as motivational tools. They also need to be comprehensible to others, including shareholders, other employees, trade unions, investor groups, even society generally, in order to help build trust and avoid suspicion. But simplicity can be dangerous because simplistic reward programmes can often have dramatic unintended consequences – consider the story of the insurance company recounted in Chapter 5 – so care is needed.

Equity incentives

Equity-based incentives should be focused on the most senior group of executives who genuinely do operate at a strategic level and who, through their decisions and actions, are capable of producing a measurable impact on firm value. Other executives and employees should have incentives which more closely align with their own departmental and individual targets and objectives. They should be given opportunities to create personal wealth through investment in company-sponsored equity plans, for example by sacrificing cash bonuses and receiving shares instead. However, these arrangements should be clearly distinguished from equity incentives, as an incentive can only incentivise if plan participants can influence the result through their own actions.

Executives should be prepared to be judged on their achievements not their efforts.

Incentives should be linked as far as possible to outputs not inputs. Shareholders cannot closely observe all the actions of executives. They cannot be sure that effort is expended in appropriate quantities, or that it is properly directed. Executives should be prepared to be judged on their achievements not their efforts. The link between achievement and creating value for the firm is more explicit than the link between value and effort. Stock options, where used, should be clearly linked to firm performance. There are many ways of doing this. More use should in future be made of indexed options, where the exercise price increases over the vesting period to take account of the company's cost of capital. Performance conditions on exercise, as commonly found among UK-quoted companies, should become the global standard. More thought should go into the actual performance criteria used. Accounting measures such as earnings per share (EPS) are only indirectly connected with growing firm value. A better measure is total shareholder return (TSR) which is, broadly speaking, the present value of all dividends and capital gains accruing to shareholders over a given period of time.

The future of share options

Share options are not the only way of providing equity incentives. Restricted share plans and performance shares, which do not automatically cease to motivate if the share price falls, can be very effective. Consideration should be given to plans which require senior executives to have some 'skin in the game', either by direct investment such as 'buy-one-get-one-free' plans, or through bonus sacrifice arrangements (surrendering part of an annual bonus in return for an award of shares).

One of the first UK companies which, in the early 1990s, decided to stop using share options as the way of providing senior executives with long-term incentives, replaced them instead with restricted shares. The company's chairman wanted to find a better way of aligning the interests of shareholders and senior executives. Working with a firm of strategy consultants he designed a long-term incentive plan under which annual awards of restricted shares were made to executive directors and certain other key employees. The extent to which awards would vest depended on the company's performance in terms of the total return to shareholders measured over a three- to five-year period. The company's TSR was compared with a group of comparator companies. TSR in each case was determined based on the internal rate of return from cash flows to an investor who bought a share at the beginning of the performance period, sold it at the end of the period, received dividends and benefited from any other capital changes during the period. There was no better way, in the opinion of the company's chairman, of putting executives into the shoes of investors.

Annual bonuses

Annual bonuses should also be part of the incentive mix. Performance criteria for annual bonuses need not all be explicitly linked to financial measures. The actions of top managers in building other types of asset, for example brands, intellectual property, organisational systems and human capital, should also feature in the scorecard. Measurement may be less precise, but performance-management systems for senior executives should be sophisticated enough to ensure that objectives are precise and success is verifiable. Line-of-sight performance standards should be used in all cases: targets must be transparent, unambiguous and understandable, and the executives must really be capable of influencing the target outcomes. Annual bonus plans should as far as possible have linear performance–pay relationships. Great care should be taken by those monitoring performance which is at or around threshold levels.

However, agency theory can never adequately explain all aspects of the relationship between shareholders and executives. In the case of the company mentioned in the example at the start of Chapter 5, the actual cost of the chief executive's bonus to an average investor owning say 5 000 shares was around £6, hardly something for *homo economicus* (the rational economic man beloved of economists) to kick up a fuss about. Even to a major shareholder, an investment fund with a 7% equity interest, the cost was only £168 000, not a huge sum on the face of it in the context of a shareholding worth around £350 000 000. Yet shareholders still felt so strongly about the chief executive's proposed bonus that they were prepared to challenge the recommendations of the remuneration committee, with far-reaching consequences for the company.

MOTIVATION CALCULUS

In order to advance our thinking about executive compensation – to progress beyond the stage of trying to design the perfect incentive contract – economic models need to be supplemented with organisational theories that relax some of the more unrealistic assumptions about human behaviour. Senior executives will have their own motivation calculus, their own set of needs and desired results. The company chairman and remuneration committee must try to understand these needs and expectations. They must understand that money is a form of calibration, a way that senior executives compare themselves with their peers. They must ensure that, notwithstanding their seniority, top managers have a proper performance management system, which should including objective setting, feedback processes and annual appraisals.

Chairmen and compensation committees should take time to understand the difference between intrinsic and extrinsic motivation. They should recognise the risk of crowding-out, when executives in effect become desensitised to normal increases in remuneration. Most importantly, chairmen and remuneration committees must understand the importance of fairness and equity between executives, and of reciprocity between top managers and shareholders. More than anything else, a corporation's remuneration systems must feel fair to the people who participate in them. The compensation committee in particular must strive to see that justice is done, but equally importantly that it is shown to be done.

A simple yet rarely used device is for companies to provide top managers with annual summaries that clearly set out the changes in their net wealth from all sources of remuneration from the firm, including stock values of equity incentive programmes and the present value of future retirement benefits. Annual compensation and benefits statements can be very motivating for other employees, and can help individuals to understand fully the cost and value implications of all aspects of their reward; why not apply the same practice to senior executives too?

CORPORATE GOVERNANCE

However well designed, incentives contracts cannot fully resolve the principal–agent problem in modern companies. Effective corporate governance is also necessary. The role of governance systems and procedures is to help manage the relationships between a company's key stakeholders, to build trust between shareholders and executives, and to ensure that companies operate by a reasonable standard of fairness. Good corporate governance can also help to avoid the escalation (unstable systems) problem described in Chapter 3.

The role of governance is to help manage the relationships between a company's key stakeholders, build trust and ensure a reasonable standard of fairness.

There are in fact two agency problems in the modern company: senior executives manage a company on behalf of all its stakeholders, particularly shareholders; shareholders in turn delegate responsibility for supervising management to a group of independent non-executive directors. If the supervisors are themselves managers or former managers, their position is compromised. This is why there is merit in the use of two-tier boards, for example a supervisory and executive board, but only if there is not an automatic progression from one to the other. The answer may be to have a main board and a separate general management committee which, like a two-tier board, clearly separates the supervisory function of the main board from the executive responsibilities of management. It is often most effective if only the CEO, or sometimes the CEO and CFO, are members of both. A significant number of large UK companies are now adopting this approach. It has been common for some time among major multinationals in Switzerland and other parts of Europe. Only in the US is the old model still frequently found, where the chairman and CEO of a company is the same person, or the chairman is a former CEO. But even in the US, companies are being encouraged to strengthen the hand of fully independent non-executive directors.

Independent chairmen and remuneration committees should take a greater role in initiating reward strategies and programmes for top management, not simply monitoring plans which have been initiated by others. One of the key responsibilities of the chairman in this split leadership model is to run the process that hires, fires, evaluates and compensates the CEO and senior management team. Remuneration committees must no longer allow themselves just to ratify management's own remuneration initiatives. To help them carry out their responsibilities, remuneration committees should ask for data directly. They should have the right (and the budgets) to hire their own expert advisers; compensation consultants, employment lawyers and so on. If one of the company's own senior HR specialists (for example the group head of compensation and benefits) is involved in designing senior executive reward policies, then it must be understood that they are being placed in a difficult position. Conflicts of interest abound. To carry out their roles effectively heads of compensation and benefits must be allowed, for this part of their work, to report directly to the company's chairman, who must in turn ensure that top management is not allowed to apply any undue pressure on any individual.

Heads of compensation and benefits must be allowed, for their senior executive reward work, to report directly to the company's chairman.

Where incentive arrangements have a significant equity component, they must be subject to very careful monitoring by the company's main board, the remuneration committee and the audit committee, who should carefully examine design and reporting issues. In carrying out their evaluations of equity incentive plans the board and audit committee need to consider proposals in the context of the company's overall relationship with investors and the capital markets generally.

And finally, the risks connected with executive reward, particularly of a failure to execute strategy, of reputation failure or of non-compliance, must be understood by directors and top managers. A risk analysis should be part of the reward design process. Each year a further risk appraisal and compliance review should be included in an annual assessment of senior executive reward strategy.

TAX AND ACCOUNTING

The tax and accounting lessons for companies and executives have been stated already. Company directors and top managers must ensure that they have a full understanding of the tax and accounting implications of reward proposals, particularly incentive plans where the greatest anomalies arise. While anomalies exist it is not unreasonable (indeed it is commercially sensible) for companies to take into account any planning opportunities as they design their reward strategies. But the tail must not wag the dog. Companies should ensure that the business objectives, particularly the desired incentive effects, are not lost in the excitement of saving tax or increasing reported profits. They should make the working assumption that accounting and tax anomalies are probably only a temporary feature of the system. It is sensible to assume that tax authorities and accounting standard setters will eventually eliminate the major anomalies and achieve a more neutral tax and accounting environment.

Company directors and top managers must ensure that they have a full understanding of the tax and accounting implications of reward proposals.

Nothing so practical as a good theory

The main principles set out in this chapter are as follows:

- The incentive contract lies at the heart of the relationship between companies and senior executives;
- An important design principle: incentive contracts must be capable of being explained (to shareholders) and understood (by executives) – beware highly complex plans!
- A senior executive's performance should be assessed by reference to observable outputs (that is, measurable achievements) not inputs (for example effort) – at this level of seniority it is actual outcomes which count;
- Equity incentives should be concentrated on the most senior group of executives – those who operate at a strategic level;
- Share options are not the only way of providing equity incentives!
- Find out what really motivates your senior people (their 'motivation calculus');
- In almost every case the felt-fair principle (for example between peers, subordinates and superiors) and reciprocity (between shareholders and executives) are central to the motivation calculus;
- Strong corporate governance (a control or negative feedback mechanism) is vital to compensate for the preponderance of positive feedback which is an inherent part of the reward design process;
- Remuneration committees should take a leading role in setting (not just monitoring) compensation policy and plans;
- When it comes to tax and accounting, do make sure that you understand the implications of your executive reward strategies, but don't let the tail wag the dog!

TURNING THEORY
INTO PRACTICE

A THEORY OF EVERYTHING

In October 2005 *The New York Times* reported on a speech given by Edgar S. Woolard, Chairman of the Compensation Committee of the New York Stock Exchange and formerly CEO of Du Pont. Like others before him, Mr Woolard was critical of pay practices for US CEOs, citing the absence of any real market, the 'top quartile' mentality (whereby every company feels it is obliged to offer its CEO target pay in the top quartile of equivalent companies), the ratcheting-up effect of pay surveys and so on. Unusually, however, Mr Woolard offered an alternative approach to CEO pay, based on his experiences at Du Pont. The solution to the executive pay problem, according to Mr Woolard, is a reward strategy known as 'internal pay equity' (IPE). It starts with an examination of the pay levels of a small number of senior managers, in Du Pont's case executives running the company's main divisions. Pay at this level should not be escalating greatly and should be capable of being readily benchmarked; there should be an effective external job market and a sufficient amount of data available to make a market pay benchmarking exercise credible. The pay of other senior executives, including the company's CEO, is then calculated by reference to this standard by applying a premium computed so as to compensate executives for the extra degree of difficulty in, effort required for, and value obtained from, these more senior roles. For example, the CEO's pay at Du Pont was set at a premium of 50% over and above the total reward of the divisional directors.

'Internal pay equity' establishes a standard and then applies a premium to senior executives' pay according to the extra degree of difficulty in their roles.

This approach is not dissimilar from the tournament model described in Chapter 3. It would be a relatively straightforward matter to enhance the sophistication of the IPE model using tournament theory. First, you would calculate the average total reward of executives operating at the highest level jobs which are capable of being benchmarked (that is, for which a credible external job market exists). Next, premiums to the benchmarked posts would be calculated using both the post-holders' reasonable expectations of future promotion and the increase that would be required to make promotion worthwhile to an executive. The CEO's total target reward, obtained by this calculation, would be split between fixed salary and benefits, a short-term incentive and a long-term incentive, for example using the ⅓: ⅓: ⅓ basis proposed for the highest levels of executive by the framework set out in Figure 3 in Chapter 2.

The attractions of this approach are that it contains an inbuilt incentive effect (see Chapter 3 for the importance of this under the principal–agent model). This is a result of the tournament theory approach to setting target total reward levels, enhanced by ensuring that an appropriate part of total reward is dependent on meeting short- and long-term performance objectives. The approach also satisfies many of the requirements of equity and fairness, given the importance placed upon internal comparisons. In this way many of the most important psychological aspects of executive pay are being addressed. Lastly, it is grounded in the external pay market, with a clear and explainable logic whereby the total reward of senior executives is built up. Shareholders, other investors and other stakeholders should be satisfied with this, particularly if the system is supported by proper performance management and an effective corporate governance framework.

THE REMUNERATION COMMITTEE'S DILEMMA

I call this 'the remuneration committee's dilemma'.

Have I answered the questions I posed in the second paragraph of Chapter 1? I hope at least the specific ones. But what of the biggest question: is it possible to reach an equilibrium point at which both senior executives and shareholders are generally satisfied and companies believe their leaders are properly incentivised? I call this 'the remuneration committee's dilemma'. It is a multi-faceted, highly complex question, as we have seen. My hope is that as a result of reading this book you will have a better understanding of the models and practices relating to senior executive reward and a clearer perspective of your own on the remuneration committee's dilemma.

UK Corporate Governance Rules for Executive Pay

GUIDING PRINCIPLES

- All listed companies are required each year to publish a directors' remuneration report with their annual accounts. This must contain a statement of the company's policy on directors' remuneration as well as individual disclosure of salaries, bonuses, pension benefits, share plans and other long-term incentives.
- Shareholders are entitled to vote on the directors' remuneration report at the company's annual general meeting, although the effect is advisory only.
- Directors' pay should be determined by a remuneration committee of the board, which should be comprised only of independent non-executive directors.
- Share options, share awards and other long-term incentive plans involving directors or the issue of new shares must be approved in advance by shareholders.
- Share incentive plans should contain demanding financial performance criteria.
- Directors' service contracts should typically not exceed one year.

SOURCES

- The Companies Act 1985, as amended by The Directors Remuneration Report Regulations 2002.
- The Listing Rules of the UK Listing Authority.
- The Combined Code on Corporate Governance, first issued by the Hampel Committee in June 1998, revised in July 2003, originally annexed to The

Listing Rules of the UK Listing Authority, and now issued by the Financial Reporting Council.

- Guidelines for institutional shareholders issued by the Association of British Insurers (ABI) and National Association of Pension Funds (NAPF).

French Corporate Governance Rules for Executive Pay

GUIDING PRINCIPLES

- French law requires all listed companies each year to publish a detailed remuneration report with their annual report and accounts. This must contain details by individual of the total compensation and benefits awarded to the company's corporate officers (*mandataires sociaux*).
- Where there is a unitary board (*conseil d'administration*) the total directors' remuneration is fixed by the shareholders' general meeting. The board of directors then determines the allocation of this amount among its members. The *Code Bouton* recommends the creation of a remuneration committee for this purpose.
- In a two-tier system the remuneration of the supervisory board (*conseil de surveillance*) is fixed by the shareholders' general meeting. The supervisory board determines the remuneration of the executive board (*directoire*). There is no obligation for the specific approval of the executive board's remuneration by shareholders.
- Golden parachutes and supplemental pension schemes for certain key executives must be approved by the company's main board and ratified by shareholders under strict 'regulated contracts' procedures.
- Every year the board of directors must submit a special report to the shareholders' general meeting concerning stock options and stock grants awarded to directors and to the top ten employees if different. Only the shareholders' general meeting has the power to authorise the award of stock options or stock grants, to set their maximum number and to determine the main conditions which apply.
- Certain key executives must report all transactions relating to their company (including share transactions) to the Financial Markets Authority (Authorités des Marchés Financiers).

- Under French law the duration of a director's service contract must not exceed six years. The second Viénot report recommends a maximum term of four years.

SOURCES

These principles are contained in:

- *Code de Commerce, Partie Législation.*
- Viénot reports, 1995 and 1999.
- Bouton report 2002.
- *Loi Breton,* 2005.
- *Règlement Général des Autorités des Marchés Financiers.*
- Principles for Corporate Governance Based on Consolidation of the 1995, 1999 and 2002 AFEP and MEDEF Reports – October 2003, issued by the Association Francaise des Entreprises Privées and Mouvement des Entreprises de France.

German Corporate Governance Rules for Executive Pay

GUIDING PRINCIPLES

- The German Corporate Governance Code recommends that listed companies should report details of the compensation paid to members of the management board in the notes to the consolidated financial statements of the company. Compensation, which should be reported on an individual basis, should be subdivided into fixed, performance-related and long-term incentive components. Companies which do not give these disclosures must disclose the fact annually.
- Since 2006 it has been a federal legal requirement that stock corporations should individually disclose details of the salaries, incentives and benefits of management board members. However, the law contains an opt-out allowing companies not to disclose individual management board remuneration if non-disclosure is approved by a 75% majority of shareholders at a general meeting.
- A dual board system is prescribed by German law for joint stock corporations. A supervisory board comprising shareholder and employee representatives oversees the activities of the management board (the *Vorstand*).
- Compensation of the members of the supervisory board shall be specified by resolution of the shareholders in a general meeting. Members of the supervisory board should review fixed- and performance-related compensation. Performance-related compensation should contain a long-term component.
- The full supervisory board should discuss and regularly review the structure of the management board's compensation system. Specific details and recommendations can be delegated to a compensation committee. Compensation of the management board shall comprise fixed salary and variable components. Variable compensation should include annual

amounts linked to business performance and long-term components containing elements of risk.

- The consolidated financial statements should contain information on stock option programmes and similar securities-based incentive schemes.
- Appointments to the supervisory board must be for a maximum of five years. Initial appointments should be for a shorter period.

SOURCES

- State Corporation Act 1965 and Securities Trading Act 1994.
- Stock Exchange Admission Regulations and Neuer Market Rules and Regulations.
- Corporate Governance study published in July 2001 by the Baum Commission.
- German Corporate Governance Code published February 2002 ('Cromme Code'), as amended May 2003.
- Vorst OG law approved by the German Federal Council in July 2005.

Swiss Corporate Governance Rules for Executive Pay

GUIDING PRINCIPLES

- Listed companies are required each year to disclose the total compensation of (a) the executive members of the board of directors and management board, in aggregate, and (b) the non-executive members of the board of directors, in aggregate. Further, without providing any names, the compensation and share and option allocations of the most highly compensated directors must be disclosed separately.
- In 2005 the Swiss parliament approved a new law which will, among other things, require listed companies to disclose, on an individual named basis, the total compensation of members of (a) the board of directors and (b) the advisory board, if any. In addition, where there is a separate executive management board, details of the total compensation of the highest-paid executive will also be required, again on an individual named basis. If enacted, this law is expected to come into force in 2007.
- A majority of the board of directors should, as a rule, be non-executives who do not perform any line management function within the company. The board will typically delegate management responsibility to a managing director and a separate executive board.
- The board of directors should set up a compensation committee, the majority of whom should comprise non-executive and independent members of the board. The compensation committee should draw up the principles for remuneration of directors and members of the executive management, and these principles should be approved by the board.
- The compensation committee should ensure that the company offers an overall package of remuneration which balances performance and market expectations. Remuneration should be demonstrably contingent upon sustainable company success.

- Details of shares and options issued to directors and executives each year must be disclosed in aggregate along with details of the number of shares held in total by (a) executive directors and members of the management board, and (b) non-executive directors.
- Transactions in company securities by members of the board of directors or executive management must be reported to the SWX Swiss Stock Exchange on a monthly basis. In the case of large individual transactions, reporting is required within two trading days; details of these transactions will be publicised by SWX on a no-names basis.
- The ordinary term of office for directors should generally not exceed four years.

SOURCES

- Swiss Code of Best Practice for Corporate Governance, issued by Economiesuisse in March 2002.
- SWX Swiss Stock Exchange Directive on Information Relating to Corporate Governance, July 2002.
- Commentary on Corporate Governance Directive, August 2004.
- SWX Swiss Stock Exchange Directive on the Disclosure of Management Transactions, July 2005.
- Swiss Code of Obligations on the Disclosure of Executive Compensation, June and October 2005.

US Corporate Governance Rules for Executive Pay

GUIDING PRINCIPLES

- All SEC registrant companies are required to file comprehensive information about their executive compensation policies and procedures. Information is disclosed to the public each year in:

  - the company's annual proxy statement;
  - the company's annual report (Form 10-K).

- Every company must disclose compensation data for their CEO and four other most highly compensated executive officers. Disclosure must include full details of base salary, bonuses, perquisites, stock options, stock awards and other long-term incentives. Executive pension plan details must also be disclosed, although in a separate table. In January 2006 the SEC put forward proposals to extend individual disclosures.

- NYSE and NASDAQ rules require that listed companies have a compensation committee composed entirely of independent directors. The compensation committee's responsibilities include assessing the CEO's performance and determining the CEO's compensation based on this evaluation, making recommendations to the board in respect to non-CEO compensation, incentive compensation plans and equity-based plans, and producing the annual compensation report required by the SEC.

- The Sarbanes Oxley Act of 2002 requires the CEO and CFO to reimburse all incentive payments and profits from sale of stock received in a year prior to an accounting restatement.

- The Internal Revenue Code sets a $1 million limit on the amount a publicly held company can claim as a corporate tax deduction in respect of compensation, payable to the CEO and each of the four other named executive officers. An important exception to the $1 million limit applies in the case of performance-based compensation awarded by the compensation committee and approved by a majority in a separate shareholder vote. A number of other conditions must be satisfied as well.

- Under the new rules companies must provide information about terms and conditions of employment contracts with the five named executive officers, including details of any compensatory arrangements for more than $100 000 which are triggered on termination of employment or change of control of the company.

SOURCES

- Securities Act of 1993, Securities Exchange Act of 1934, and SEC regulations relating thereto, in particular item 402 of Regulation S-K.
- Sarbanes-Oxley Act of 2002.
- Listing rules of the New York Stock Exchange, NASDAQ and other securities exchanges.
- Guidelines set by certain influential shareholder groups and investment advisers, such as CalPERS and Institutional Shareholder Services (ISS).

Further Reading

Kevin J. Murphy of the Marshall Business School, University of Southern California, is probably the leading academic commentator on executive remuneration, and this book is heavily indebted to his thinking. He has written variously by himself, and with Michael C. Jensen, Brian J. Hall and others. His June 1999 paper entitled 'Executive Compensation' provides an excellent summary of previous academic writing on the subject. It can be found in the *Handbook of Labor Economics*, edited by Orley Ashenfelter and David Card. More recently he has issued, with Michael J. Jensen, an updated review of the literature called 'Remuneration: Where We've Been, How We've Got Here, What Are The Problems, and How to Fix Them'. This was published in July 2004 by the European Corporate Governance Institute as one of their finance working papers (Reference No 44/2004).

A different approach to the question of executive remuneration is found in *Pay Without Performance: The Unfilled Promise of Executive Compensation* by Lucian Bebchuk and Jesse Fried, respectively of Harvard Law School and the law school at the University of California, Berkeley. Their thesis is that top managers use their positions to extract rents disguised as incentive pay, and that governance processes are not a match for executive power.

A review of Bebchuk and Fried's book by William W. Bratton of the Georgetown University Law Center, Columbia Law School, called 'The Academic Tournament over Executive Pay' published in the *California Law Review* Vol. 93, No. 5, 2005 provides a helpful summary of the position of Bebchuk and Fried, on the one hand, and Kevin J. Murphy and associates, on the other. Bratton comes down in favour of Bebchuk and Fried although, as you will have understood from this book, I do not necessarily agree with him.

A very good graduate-level summary of compensation theory can be found in *Compensation: Theory, Evidence, and Strategic Implications* by Barry Gerhart and Sara L. Rynes (Sage Publications, 2003).

A non-technical introduction to game theory can be found in *Game Theory at Work* by James Miller of Smith College, published by McGraw-Hill in 2003.

John Roberts, who holds the John H. and Irene S. Scully Professorship in Economics, Strategic Management, and International Business at the Graduate School of Management of Stanford University, is one of the current leading thinkers on organisational theory, which includes the application of principal–agent theory to the management of companies. His book, *The Modern Firm – Organisational Design for Performance and Growth*, published by Oxford University Press in 2004, provides an excellent introduction to principal–agent theory, among other things.

Good books on motivation and senior executives' behaviour are hard to find. I have used Charles Handy's *Understanding Organisations*, first published by Penguin Books in 1973. This still contains one of the best summaries of psychologists' thinking about motivation, as well as proposing the motivation calculus as a way of bringing various diverse theories together. A more recent summary of motivation theories can be found in *Organisational Behaviour 1: Essential Theories of Motivation and Leadership* by John B. Milner, published by M.E. Sharpe, Armonk, New York, in 2005.

Alexander Pepper ESRC/FME Fellow
Department of Management, The London School of Economics
and Political Science, Houghton Street, London WC2A 2AE
Tel: +44 (0)20 7106 1208 Mob: +44 (0)7590 077165
e-mail: a.a.pepper@lse.ac.uk

18/2/09.

Dear Jo,

Many thanks for sending me "Think Ages"
(good title). I'm afraid the enclosed is not so
exciting, but I thought I would send you a
copy anyway.

Look forward to seeing you on 16 April!

Best wishes.

Andy.

Index